AN ANTHOLO 200 SCRIPTURE-BASED DECREES AND PRAYERS FOR SONS

Shaping the Lives and Future of School Boys, Teenage Guys and Young Adult Men at University and Beyond

VUYI BOATENG

Copyright © 2023 Vuyi Boateng
All rights reserved.

No part of this publication may be reproduced, stored in a retrieval system, distributed or transmitted in any form or by any means (electronic, mechanical, photocopying, recording, or otherwise) without prior written permission from the publisher.

The author makes reasonable efforts to present accurate and reliable information in this book; The author is not responsible for any errors in or omissions references or websites listed or other information contained in this book.

TABLE OF SUBJECT AREAS

Fulfilment Of Prophetic Words 1
Worthiness 2
Daily Victory 3
Calling 4
Advancement 5
Academic Stamina 6
Help And Assistance 7
Personal Focus 8
Wisdom 9
Mind Renewal 10
Empowerment 11
Good Works 12
Support 13
Anointing For Success 14
Miracles 15
All Round Blessing 16
More Blessings 17
God's Love 18
A Bright Future 19
Academic Learning And Retention 20
Angelic Ministration 21
Attention 22
Access To Good 23
Prayerfulness 24
Skill 25

Victory	26
Divine Selection	27
Bravery And Strength	28
Elevation	29
Ease	30
Triumph	31
Honesty	32
Salvation	33
Daily Improvement	34
Predestination	35
Enablement	36
Honour	37
Meekness	38
Confidence	39
Focus	40
Comfort	41
Power	42
Diligence	43
Freedom	44
Networks	45
Help	46
Greatness	47
Fulfilment	48
God's Perfection	49
Deliverance	50
Benevolence	51
Faith	52
Academic Teachability	53
Grace	54
Strength	55
Anointing	56
Plans	57
Light	58
Intelligence	59
Forward Planning	60

Humility	61
Alertness	62
Attention	63
Godly Passion	64
Social Standing	65
Increase	66
Perseverence	67
Liberty	68
Progress	69
Godly Destiny	70
Praise Worthiness	71
Belief	72
Favour	73
Celebration	74
God's Presence	75
God's Faithfulness	76
Stature	77
Academic Focus	78
Altitude	79
Brilliance	80
Giftedness	82
Steadfastness	83
Nobility	84
Promotion	85
Eminence	86
Revelation	87
Gratification	88
Momentum	89
Resilience	90
Uprightness	91
Honesty	92
Health	93
Skill	94
Benediction	95
Gracefulness	96

Insight	97
Virtue	98
Dominion	99
Enjoyment	100
Security	101
Effort	102
Divinity	103
Friendships	104
Divine Love	105
Divine Knowledge	106
Ascendancy	107
Advantage	108
Compliance	109
Integrity	110
Godliness	111
Abundant Life	112
Ordination	113
Might	114
Prosperity	115
Brightness	116
Forgiveness	117
Redemption	118
Counsel	119
Transformation	120
Model Behaviour	121
Preservation	122
Christ Mindedness	124
Protection	125
Peacefulness	126
Authority	127
Providence	128
Liberation	129
Ordination	130
His Intellect	131
Good Relationships	132

Providence	133
Pre-Determination	134
Thoughts	135
Honour	136
Best Results	137
Protection	138
Preservation	139
God's Presence	140
Pride Worthiness	141
Character	142
Piety	143
Defence	144
Godly Alignment	145
Benevolence	146
Virtue	147
Potency	148
Praise For The Lord	149
Divine Nature	150
Conquest	151
Predestination	152
Giftedness	153
Honour	154
Goal Getting	155
Closeness To God	156
Positive Speech	157
Guidance	158
Welfare	159
Faith	160
Godly Passion	161
Security	162
Enhancement	163
Blessed Works	164
Uniqueness	165
Excellence	166
Expansion And Growth	167

Ability	168
Renewal	169
Excess	170
Devoutness	171
Understanding	172
Conquest	173
Ordination	174
Prayer	175
Testimonials	176
Divine Success	177
Insight	178
Support	179
Illumination	180
Provision	181
Biblical Knowledge	182
Liberation	183
Endeavour	184
Carefulness	185
Personal Godliness	186
Conscience	187
Will	188
Purpose	189
Mental Health	190
God's Counsel	191
Spiritual Sonship	192
Spiritual Fruitfulness	193
Peace	194
Soul	195
Spirit	196
Path	197
Life	198
Comfort	199
Mercy	200

GLOSSARY

The scriptures in this book have been gathered from different versions and translations of the Bible and these are condensed into acronyms. For ease of understanding and reference, the versions and their abbreviations are as follows:

NIV	New International Version
KJV	King James Version
NKJV	New King James Version
GNT	Good News Translation
ESV	English Standard Version
NLT	New Living Translation
CSB	Christian Standard Bible
NASB	New American Standard Bible

ACKNOWLEDGEMENTS

This anthology could not have been completed had it not been for several key people who consciously or unconsciously coached me into completing it and supported the vision. I am grateful for my family for being instrumental in helping me identify each of the subject areas covered herein. All those who agreed to debate, discuss, edit and pray about this book will always hold a special place in my heart. I am excited to see how the lives of sons all over the world will be transformed.

DEDICATION

This anthology is dedicated to the mothers and fathers, grandparents, churches, teachers, god-parents, aunties and uncles, intercessory prayer groups and coaches who have a special love for sons all over the world.

PREFACE

This is a book about sons. They need special prayers and attention not least because of societal expectations but also because they are a special target spiritually. While there is a tendency amongst some Christians to always think positively, the enemy is unapologetically and strategically attacking the male gender as a means of destabilising families and society at large. It is important to recognise this and to develop strategies on how to combat the devices of Satan. This is why this anthology of scriptures, decrees and prayers to be said over sons is vital in today's 21st century reality.

There is no question that daughters are equally important - having also been created in the image and likeness of God, they are as valuable and deserving of positive attention as sons. In current society though: boys, male adolescents, young male university students and young male adults face unparalleled circumstances and challenges. This books contains only 200 of the subject areas that require special attention in a son's life. Some of them are about the development of the attitude, behaviour, and character of a son. Others pertain to his mind-set and mental health as well as his decisions and emotions. The book also deals with the physical health and the role of a son in his school, his community, and his church. Prayers about achievement, attainment, ambition, and the building blocks that create a successful man are also included. Careful attention is also given to the spiritual gifts, divine calling and matters of the soul of every son. These are issues that affect all children but they are experientially different for boys.

Some boys are conditioned to suppress their emotions unlike girls, hence the adage "boys don't cry". This emotional suppression could later on foster a lack of emotional intelligence and a poor emotional quotient when they mature into men. Linked to this is the development of frustration and unresolved anger that can turn boys into men who use violence solve issues. The pseudoscientific concept of the Alpha Male can also raise unique issues based on the male need to be a commander, visionary, strategist and executor.

These traits can foster a bullying culture where some boys intimidate, harass and assault other boys as well as girls. Boys at the receiving end can be damaged while the offenders could start the course to toxic masculinity. This is why work place bullying has become a corporate concern. Academic attainment and cognitive issues can also be challenging for boys because according to some World Health Organisation statistics the prevalence of Attention Deficit Hyperactivity Disorder and Autism Spectrum Disorder is several times more in males than it is in females.

The adolescence phase can be particularly challenging too. Boys face added pressure to look a certain way in terms of height and muscle build. While girls can simply wear make-up, use cosmetics and wear high heels, some boys can start to develop body confidence issues if they are not built like those they see on social media. Some of them can be pressurised to be "cool" and "be a man" and sometimes this involves being forced to defy parents, drink alcohol or take drugs as a means of proving that they are in control and not a "mama's boy". The desire to belong and to be led, especially in boys who have been brought up by single mothers, could lead some to join a gang led by a strong and dominant male figure. Physically, the endocrine system also places more hormonal pressure on the sex drive of adolescent boys than it does on girls. Adolescence also involves increased developmental processes regarding the brain and the Limbic system that controls emotional responses. If a teenage boy did not learn how to control his emotions, he can become particularly confused, subdued and distant during this time. Those emotions that were suppressed during boyhood, such as anger and sadness can begin to manifest. If this is in the form of depression and anxiety, it can be particularly difficult for the male gender as it can more easily lead to alcohol and drug abuse.

Another set of challenges awaits those that make it to university. Bad company corrupts good morals and if a boy joins the wrong crowd, he could end up partying and drinking with "the guys" and having sex instead of remaining focused and steady so as to finish his studies on time. Finally, biologically, the frontal lobe in the brain closes later in males than it does in females. It only matures at the age of 25 in males and has an impact on thinking, emotions, personality, judgment, and self-control, amongst other things.

So, from the first day of school until university graduation day, boys need special prayers. This is not to say that girls and young ladies experience none of these issues. It is simply to say that boys and young men experience issues differently because modern day society places patriarchal pressure on males. This is why deliberate, and focused prayer efforts need to be made for them.

It is instinctive for every normal parent to want to be physically present around their son at all times. The day that we drop them off on the first day at primary school is when we realise that no parent can be with their child in the classroom, the playground, the athletic field or in an examination, test or assessment. We are not able to choose friends for them either. But, as Christians, there are three things that we can always be sure of.

Firstly, the spirit of the Lord is omnipresent – He accompanies our children wherever they go. This intimate nearness of the Lord is described in Psalm 139:7-12 where the Psalmist says:

> "Where could I go from Your Spirit? Or where could I flee from Your presence?
> If I ascend up into heave, You are there; if I make my bed in Sheol (the place of the dead), behold, You are there.
> If I take the wings of the morning or dwell in the uttermost parts of the sea,
> Even there shall Your hand lead me, and Your right hand shall hold me.
> If I say, Surely the darkness shall cover me and the night shall be the light about me.
> Even the darkness hides nothing from you, but the night shines as the day; the darkness and light are both alike to You."

The Lord will therefore always be present wherever our sons are!

Secondly, there is infinite power in the words that we speak. Even non-Christians are cautious and realise that words can become a "self-fulfilling prophecy". This simply means that an individual's expectations about another person or entity could eventually be confirmed in reality. Put differently, a set of beliefs can positively or negatively influence outcomes. It may sound esoteric, but the psychological phenomena relating to the Placebo and

Pygmalion effects are based on the concept of a self-fulfilling prophecy, hence we need to be careful what we say.

For the Christian, there is Biblical precedent, set in Job 22:28 that a man "shall decree a thing and the light of God shall shine upon its way." In other words, whatever we say will come to light and life. This is true for positive and negative words alike. Some parents are guilty of using negative language in the process of correcting their children. For example, a parent might say "you will not amount to anything in life" as a means of scaring their child into studying for exams or taking a more serious approach to life. As Christians, it is important for us to realise that our expectations will not be cut off. Indeed, it is made clear in Matthew 12:36 and 37 and Proverbs 18:7 that a foolish man can be condemned and ensnared by his words and that each person will be called to give account for every careless word spoken. If you are a parent that is struggling to believe that your son will succeed in life, this book will help you change and shift your mind-set and help you believe for better things and thus create a more positive outcome for your family. This book will help us all to speak declarative words that can follow our children where we cannot go and create the realities that we would like to see.

The third thing we can be sure of as Christians is that the word of God carries an innate and unrivalled power that is creative and transformative. Indeed, Hebrews 4:12 tells us that the words of God are alive, quick and swift, sharp, active and effective. Jesus Christ said that His words are spirit and they are life in John 6:63. Genesis 1 demonstrates this because our creator spoke what He wanted to see and it manifested. Our words can travel through space and guard our sons. They can travel through time into the future and meet with our sons on arrival.

HOW TO USE THIS BOOK

This book is intended for mothers and fathers, grandparents and extended family, churches and prayer groups who are interested in the welfare of boys, teenage boys, and young men. It is also for people who wish to exercise their faith regarding sons that are yet to be born or baby boys. The parents of girls can also pray and speak over their future sons-in-law. The contents of the book are intended to be read out loudly, authoritatively and imaginatively with a picture of the desired outcome in mind.

Each page is divided into 3 sections that cover a particular topic.

First, read out the special scripture that is stated - it has been chosen because of its relevance to the topic. The page starts with the word of God because it is immutable and embodies His will for us. Every word of God is didactic and has the power to influence situations: it is alive. It has the power to create, fashion and form. This is why Psalm 138:2 says that our God has exalted his word even above his name!

Next, say the decree. Loosely translated, a decree is an order that has the force of law. Biblically, decrees were issued by kings and most of them were irrevocable. On the basis of both 1 Peter 2:9 and revelations 1:6, those who believe in Christ are kings and priests and He is the King of kings. With this in mind, adopt your position as a king and a priest and pronounce the decree - it is a carefully chosen authoritative statement on the topic you will be focusing on for your son. These decrees are bold and unapologetic mandates made as a matter of fact, regardless of the current situation. They should be spoken in faith because faith is a fierce and powerful force that can literally move proverbial mountains. Hence, the Bible says if anyone has faith they can speak to and command a mountain to move and be cast into the sea and it will obey (Mark 11:23). By faith, we can speak out words and see them materialise in physical form.

Lastly, say the prayer. James 5:16 states that the effective and fervent prayer of a righteous person avails much. Therefore it is best for you to forgive all that have hurt you, set your spirit aright and adopt the right spiritual posture before saying the prayer. Besides containing special areas of intercession for your son, the prayer on each page synchronizes the decree and the scripture that you would have made on that page.

> *An important final word is that the utterances included in the book are not meant to paint a picture of a perfect son. They are not intended to distress sons and their parents into thinking that a flawless son has to emerge out of them. They are simply to assist those who love sons to create the best life they can. It is my strong belief that, together, every vocalised scripture, decree and prayer will result in the enhancement, improvement and betterment of the life of every son in your heart and mind. I pray that like a symphony, the scriptures, decrees and prayers in this book will combine to make sons into stronger, well-rounded, resilient, and brilliant people who know their God and do mighty exploits as promised in Daniel 11:32b.*

1

FULFILMENT OF PROPHETIC WORDS

Job 22:28
Thou shalt also decree a thing and it shall be established unto thee and the light of God shall shine upon thy ways. (KJV)

MY DECREE

Every decree I make is established here and now without delay. I assert that my son is self-assured. He affirms only good things about himself. His teachers, peers, coaches and everyone he interacts with speak well of him. As I speak the word of God, I express His will and everything I ask in the name of Jesus Christ is established in my sons life, according to God's good pleasure.

MY PRAYER

Dear Lord,
I thank you that you have empowered us to issue decrees and speak things forth for we are kings and priests (Ecclesiastes 8:4 and 1 Peter 2:9).
By your grace and love, every positive prophecy spoken over my son by me and others that love him becomes a reality through the power of the Holy Spirit.
AMEN.

WORTHINESS

2 Thessalonians 1:11-12
With this in mind, we constantly pray for you, that our God may make you worthy of his calling, and that by his power he may bring to fruition your every desire for goodness and every deed prompted by faith. We pray this so that the name of our Lord Jesus may be glorified in you, and you in him, according to the grace of God and Lord Jesus Christ. (NIV)

MY DECREE

My son is called to achieve extra-ordinary things in his generation. He leads his peers. He lives an exemplary life that others seek to emulate. Every hope of the Lord for my son is being achieved at the right time, with the right help and in the right way. My son walks in his prophetic calling daily.

MY PRAYER

Dear Father,
I thank you for the calling that you have issued on my son's life. I thank you that he answers it faithfully and timeously. Thank you for the measure of faith that you have given him for the fulfilment of your call. I thank you for the grace and faith you have granted him (1 Corinthians 12:9) and that by this, he makes advancements in your kingdom and in life.
AMEN.

3

DAILY VICTORY

Psalm 68:19
Blessed be the Lord, who daily loads us with benefits, the God of our salvation. (NKJV)

MY DECREE

Through the grace of the Lord Jesus Christ, the accomplishments of my son are noteworthy and they cause him to stand as a leader. He is empowered to prosper daily. He is capacitated, tenacious and determined to achieve and accomplish goal to the point of prosperous completion and success.

MY PRAYER

Our Father, I thank you for always placing my son at an advantage in all he is involved in. I am confident that by your grace, everyday yields positive results of attainment and dominion for him. I am grateful for all the favourable results of an overcomer that are in his life.
AMEN.

CALLING

2 Timothy 3:17
...that the servant of God may be thoroughly equipped for every good work. (NIV)

MY DECREE

By the grace of God, my son is adequately prepared to meet every demand placed on him.
Through positive effort, skill and courage, my son is fulfilling, establishing and securing great success in all that he is involved in. He is anointed and endowed with the spiritual power to carry out positive works daily.

MY PRAYER

Lord Jesus Christ, I thank you that your virtue and righteousness follow and surround my son wherever he goes, whatever he is involved in and through all his interactions. Thank you that you are reflected in him and that all areas of his life are blessed.
AMEN.

5

ADVANCEMENT

Psalm 18:29
With your help, I can advance against a troop; with my God I can scale a wall. (NIV)

MY DECREE

Through the assistance of the Lord Jesus Christ, the power of the Lord accelerates the manifestation of my son's greatness.
His mental, spiritual and all round growth and development are quickened. His trajectory is upward. He takes giant leaps and pursues, expedites and promotes his God-ordained destiny. With ease, he is going the long haul academically, spiritually and physically.

MY PRAYER

Our Father, I thank you that you strengthen and embolden my son. Thank you that through you, he is subduing all challenges, situations, issues and difficulties that he may face at every stage. By your grace, his way is made perfect. Thank you that your strength enables him to achieve unprecedented things in his life.
AMEN.

6

ACADEMIC STAMINA

Isaiah 40:31
But those who hope in the Lord shall renew their strength; they shall mount up with wings as eagles; they shall run, and not be weary: they will walk, and not be faint. (KJV)

MY DECREE

My son is progressing in all areas of his life. He makes advancements academically and in faith, maturity and purpose. He moves forward and makes headway in all his endeavours. He forges ahead and draws nearer to the attainment of his goals and those set for him. My son surpasses countless milestones and continues to advance daily.

MY PRAYER

Lord, I thank you that my son will always have a positive expectation and desire for good. By the grace of our Lord Jesus Christ, I am confident that his hopes will mature into a faith that will avail much in all areas of his life.
AMEN.

7

HELP AND ASSISTANCE

Isaiah 41:10
So do not fear, for I am with you; do not be dismayed, for I am your God. I will strengthen you and help you; I will uphold you with my righteous right hand. (NIV)

MY DECREE

The Lord Himself, angels, key people and resources are on hand to assist my son at any and every point of need. My son lives in peace and comfort, health and longevity. Abundant finances are meeting all his needs at all times. The key people that are needed in order to take my son to his destiny are willing, available and accessible to him.

MY PRAYER

In the name of Jesus Christ, I thank you Lord that your presence brings aid, assistance and relief to my son at all times. Thank you that your help raises his confidence and self-image so that he always feels supported. Thank you that through you, he does all things fear-lessly.
AMEN.

PERSONAL FOCUS

1 Corinthians 9:24
Do you not know that in a race all the runners run, but only one gets the prize? Run in such a way that you may obtain it.
(NKJV)

MY DECREE

My son is self-disciplined and focused at all times. He concentrates well on all he is taught and on all he needs to learn. He is also self-controlled and alert. This all brings positive results in all areas of his life.

MY PRAYER

Heavenly Father I thank you that your Spirit is always encouraging my son and spurring him on to the mark of his higher calling.
Thank you that he is attentive to you. Thank you that my son accomplishes all that you have set aside for him to do in his youth and beyond. Thank you that he is achieving mastery at every level of life.
AMEN.

WISDOM

Proverbs 4:7
Wisdom in the principal thing; therefore get wisdom: and with all thy getting get understanding. (KJV)

MY DECREE

My son is gifted with the spirit of wisdom and he understands and retains all the good things that he is taught. Through prudence and a grace for excellence, he is working to produce brilliant results.

The spirit of the Lord abides in my son and unlocks spiritual growth and the knowledge of God for his daily living. By the enlightenment of the Lord my son exhibits an excellent and teachable spirit. He achieves all round success in all things.

MY PRAYER

Lord Jesus Christ, I thank you for showing my son how to be sensible and wise even as he goes through the challenges of youth. Grant him knowledge and experiences that will set him apart amongst his generation. Thank you that he is born to lead. Thank you for fostering and perfecting this gift of governance and leadership in him at all stages of his life.
AMEN.

10

MIND RENEWAL

Romans 12:2
And be not be conformed to this world: but be transformed by the renewing of your mind, that ye may prove what is that good, and acceptable, and perfect, will of God.
(KJV)

MY DECREE

My son stands out positively in any and all situations. His mind is constantly adapting appropriately to new material, no matter how challenging it may appear to be. My son accepts the unique call of God on his life and his life adapts to the word of God.

MY PRAYER

Most High God, I thank you that my son is unique. Thank you that he is consecrated
for greatness. By faith I declare that my son is using the
unique gifts you have placed in him to serve the world around him. Thank you that by the work of the holy spirit that you have placed in him, my son is overcoming all challenges.
AMEN.

11

EMPOWERMENT

Acts 1:8
But you will receive power when the holy spirit comes upon you. (NIV)

MY DECREE

The Holy Spirit dwells inside of my son. My son was sealed with the Holy Spirit when he accepted the gift of salvation. Therefore, through the Holy Spirit, my son received enabling power to remove, uproot and destroy anything that is not of God's glory in all areas of his life. The power of the Holy Spirit is more powerful than any other power that can come against my son.

MY PRAYER

Abba Father,
Thank you that the same power that raised Jesus Christ from the dead is in my son (Romans 8:11). Thank you that you are able to do exceedingly, abundantly and above all I can ask, think or imagine for my son, in accordance with this power that is at work in him (Ephesians 3:20). Thank you that my son is blessed with uncommon abilities and strengths that he can rely on daily
AMEN.

12

GOOD WORKS

2 Corinthians 9:8
And God is able to make all grace abound to you, that ye, always having all sufficiency in all things, may abound to every good work. (KJV)

MY DECREE

By the grace of God, my son is excelling in all areas of his life and work. He is using power, skills, means and opportunities to accomplish outstanding results at all times. My son uses the proficiency, intelligence, brilliance, capability and gifts necessary for practical all-round success in all aspects of his life.

MY PRAYER

Dear Lord Jesus Christ, thank you for your mercy and kindness towards my son. By faith, I declare that he is ever fruitful at all times because of your hand upon him. Thank you that your presence empowers his life to overflow with good works and great achievements.
AMEN.

13

SUPPORT

Psalm 63:7
Because thou hast been my help, therefore in the shadow of your wings, I rejoice. (KJV)

MY DECREE

My son receives the right and appropriate, patient and attentive aid that he requires at all times. He meets with the right people who have been empowered by God to bless him in the areas that he needs assistance. The Lord helps me as a parent to fulfil my own destiny in my son's life. My role is facilitated by the spirit of the Lord. The right helpers of my son's destiny are willing and able to work out their purpose in his life.

MY PRAYER

Thank you Holy Spirit that you are my son's personal helper (John 14:26). Thank you Lord that you have given your angels charge over him to keep him in all his ways and to help him in all that he does (Psalm 91:11). Thank you that because of this, my son is a blessing.
AMEN.

14

ANOINTING FOR SUCCESS

Jeremiah 22:29
O earth, earth, earth, hear the word of the LORD. (KJV)

MY DECREE

The Earth is yielding its best experiences and solutions for my son. I am thankful that my son's life on Earth is blessed by God. The Lord has anointed him with power and uncommon ability through Christ. My son is realising his talents, gifts and callings. The angels of the Lord perpetually announce good news about my son to me and the world around us.

MY PRAYER

Thank you Lord that the Earth has been given to man as an inheritance (Psalm 115:16). Thank you that the Earth is ours to subdue and that I have been given dominion and authority over it (Genesis 1:28). By faith, I declare that all the kingdoms of the Earth, all of its structures and the things that are in place to bless man on the Earth will honour and be expressed in my son. Thank you that in the name of the Lord Jesus Christ, the Earth shall yield its increase to my son.
AMEN.

MIRACLES

1 Corinthians 1:27
But God chose the foolish things of this world to confound the wise, and God hath chosen the weak things of the world to confound the things which are mighty. (KJV)

MY DECREE

The Lord uses the mundane and seemingly unremarkable things to elevate my son. I am astounded by the power of God that is at work in my son's life. This force and energy turns all negative and impossible situations around. No matter how foolish and weak things may seem, they work in the favour of my son. I thank God for the development of physical, mental, emotional and spiritual growth in him. I dedicate him back to the Lord and miracles continue to happen.

MY PRAYER

I thank you, Lord, that only your word, which is forever settled in heaven (Psalm 119:89) will avail much in my son's life. I thank you, Lord, that no negative word that is contrary to your Word about my son will come to reality in his life. I thank you that at Your word every negative promise and prophecy about my son will have no effect. Thank you Lord that you orchestrate everything, even the foolish and simplistic things, in conformity to your will for my son.
AMEN.

16

ALL ROUND BLESSING

Deuteronomy 28:3-14
The fruit of your womb will be blessed, and the crops of your land and the young of your livestock – the calves of your herds and the lambs of your flocks. Your basket and your kneading trough will be blessed. You will be blessed when you come in and when you go out. (NIV paraphrased)

MY DECREE

From whichever angle he is looked at, my son is blessed. Whichever way I examine his life, he is prospering physically, mentally, academically, emotionally, spiritually and in his soul. My sons achievements are considerable for his age. He is blessed with understanding and this is evident in all he does. This is my heritage in Christ and it manifests in my life.

MY PRAYER

Our Lord and our Saviour, I thank you that you have blessed my son with everything that he needs pertaining to life and godliness (2 Peter 1:3). Thank you for your promise that, because he is the fruit of my womb and seed of my loins, he is a righteous reward and an inheritance to the nations in his generation. By your grace, my son is blessed on every side because of your grace, favour, mercy and love.
AMEN.

17

MORE BLESSINGS

Deuteronomy 28:6
You will be blessed when you come and when you go out.
(NIV)

MY DECREE

My son is honoured in all walks of life and accepted by everyone. He does not labour in vain. Rather, he is rewarded for all his hard work, time spent and efforts. Favour, blessing and divine recognition constantly follow and are expressed in him. His gifts and talents are recognised, nurtured, developed and awarded accordingly. He is enabled and empowered to prosper.

MY PRAYER

Father, I thank you that you teach my son to profit and that you lead him in the paths that he should follow (Isaiah 48:17). I pray that my son works wisely, smartly and with wisdom because the blessing of the Lord makes rich and adds no painful toil (Proverbs 10:22). I humbly ask that you increase my son's work ethic and that you enable him to autograph all of his work with excellence.
AMEN.

18

GOD'S LOVE

Psalm 46:8
Come and see what the Lord has done, the amazing things he has done on the Earth. (GNT)

MY DECREE

I am astonished by the works of God in my son's life. They are evident in his academics, his comportment and relationships. The power of God amazes me because it transforms his learning and life experiences. I am astounded by God's effective influence over my sons mind, heart, souls and emotions. By the grace and power of God, my son is a leader amongst his peers and he makes history from an early age.

MY PRAYER

Heavenly Father, I testify in advance of the good things that you have done for and through my son's life. I thank you that he is prospered, enabled and victorious at every stage and level of his life. Thank you for decorating his life with abundant blessing and testimony.
AMEN.

19

A BRIGHT FUTURE

Jeremiah 29:11
For I know that plans I have for you says the Lord, plans to prosper you and not to harm you, plans to give you hope and a future. (NIV)

MY DECREE

The Lord has already arranged a bright future for my son: at school, at home, at church, in public, in private, on the sports field and in all areas of his life. Every plan, divine appointment and encounter that the Lord has pre-destined over my son's life materialises on time.
All the good things that the Lord has arranged for my son in advance lead to positive and powerful experiences.

MY PRAYER

Almighty God, I thank you that you no eye has seen, no ear has heard and no mind has conceived what you have in store for my son (1 Corinthians 2:9). Thank you that you knew him before he was conceived (Jeremiah 1:5). Thank you for the future that you have planned for him. I already rejoice over it, by faith.
Thank you that many are the plans in a man's heart but it is only your purposes and rich plans over him that will prosper (Proverbs 19:21).
AMEN.

ACADEMIC LEARNING AND RETENTION

Psalm 32:8
I will instruct you and teach you in the way you should go; I will counsel you with my loving eye on you. (NIV)

MY DECREE

My son is assimilating all that he has been taught, with ease. His mind learns, processes and comprehends all examinable material and he excels in his studies. Through extraordinary retentive abilities, he calls all relevant material to remembrance during oral, written and practical examinations. Importantly, the word of God is in my son's memory, his conscious and subconscious mind. By faith, he is drawn closer to the Lord and meditates on the true word of God.

MY PRAYER

Thank you Jesus Christ that there is an anointing that my son received when he accepted you as his personal saviour (1 John 2:27). Thank you that because of the breath of the Almighty that is in man and gives understanding (Job 32:8), my son is prospering in all seasons and at all times in his mind, body, soul and spirit. By faith, I decree and declare that this is reflected in all of his circumstances.
AMEN

21

ANGELIC MINISTRATION

Hebrews 1:14
Are not angels ministering spirits sent to serve those who will inherit salvation? (NIV)

MY DECREE

The angels of the Lord minister to my son. They make sure he is protected and they guard his life. They deliver blessings from the Lord into his life and make sure that his foot does not slip. My son receives glad tidings, news of his consecration and confirmation about the Lords call on his life from the angels of the Lord. They maintain portals of communication between my son and the throne of God and this is a normal occurrence for him.

MY PRAYER

Our Father and our God, I thank you that you are the Lord of hosts. Thank you that the heavenly hosts fight on our behalf and ensure that our feet do not slip. Thank you that my son is firmly guarded by angels and that his life is daily filled with angelic ministration and visitation. I thank you that your angels are there to ensure that your will in his life is done. Thank you that he is protected from all evil, according to your word (Matthew 6:13).
AMEN.

ATTENTION

Job 32:8
But there is a spirit in man, And the breath of the Almighty gives him understanding. (NIV)

MY DECREE

By the grace of the Lord Jesus Christ, my son understands all things that require his attention. By this knowledge and astuteness, my son is blessed in all of his ways. He is achieving his God-given and predestined purpose in life. He does so early and lives in a realm of destiny fulfilment.

MY PRAYER

Lord Jesus Christ, I thank you for the intellectual and emotional strength you have given my son.
Thank you that the mind of Christ is at work in him and his achievements at every stage are praiseworthy.
AMEN.

23

ACCESS TO GOOD

Isaiah 45:2
I will go before you and make the crooked places straight; I will break in pieces the gates of brass, and cut in sunder the bars of iron. And I will give thee the treasures of darkness, and hidden tiches of secret places, that thou mayest know that I, the LORD, which call thee by name, am the God of Israel. (KJV)

MY DECREE

My son is granted divine access to amazing opportunities by the Lord. These follow him all the days of his life. My son accesses the assistance he needs as and when he needs it. He is connected to the indwelling Holy Spirit as well as the wisdom and knowledge of God. He thrives in a relationship with Christ.

MY PRAYER

Our Lord, I thank you that all things and all the people of the Earth belong to you (Psalm 24:1). Thank you that you have commissioned people, places, opportunities and all things under your power to bless my son. Thank you that he has an uncommon and Godly heritage in Christ.
AMEN.

24

PRAYERFULNESS

1 Thessalonians 5:16-19
Rejoice evermore, pray without ceasing. In everything give thanks: for this is the of God in Christ Jesus concerning you.
(KJV)

MY DECREE

My son has a can-do and can-be attitude that is always effective in all areas of life. His attitude towards his studies and the things of God is always pleasing. Due to his good character and excellent behaviour, my son accesses great opportunities at all stages of his life. He makes history from a young age.

MY PRAYER

Our Father and our Lord, in all circumstances, good and bad, positive and negative, through trials and triumphs: I thank you for your work in the life of my son. Thank you for gracing us with the ability to praise, pray and give thanks without ceasing. Thank you that no matter how things may seem, you always answer all of our prayers and petitions (Philippians 4:6) through the power, wisdom, glory and love.
AMEN.

SKILL

Exodus 31:3 I have filled him with the Spirit of God, in wisdom, in understanding, in knowledge, and in all manner of workmanship. (KJV)

MY DECREE

My son is acquiring great skill and knowledge about all things that are necessary for him to have a good life. He obtains an excellent education by God-given wisdom and through the Word of God. The result is great prosperity in his health, finances, abilities, academic studies and chosen vocation.

PRAYER

Thank you Lord that you are involved in all the circumstances of our lives. Thank you that you have given my son all that he needs for life and godliness, victory and peace, success and triumph in all circumstances. Thank you that my son is wise, knowledgeable and taught by your spirit (Isaiah 54:13).
AMEN.

VICTORY

Matthew 18:18
Truly I tell you, whatever you bind on earth will be bound in heaven, and whatever you loose on earth will be loosed in heaven. (NIV)

MY DECREE

With the keys to the kingdom of our Father that I have been given, I unlock all the good things that the Lord has prepared for my son. I release the opportunities that the Lord has pre-destined for my son, into his life. Everything that is good and perfect comes from the Lord and I bind it to my son. I loose anything that is not of the glory of the Lord from his life, and him from it. I disallow everything that is working against my son and is loses its influence over him. My son prospers well in all areas of his life.

MY PRAYER

Dear Lord,
Thank you that through the power you have given me, I can loose all things that are not of your glory from the life of my son. As I do so here on earth, you are carrying it out in heaven at the same time. Thank you that all good things that life and wisdom have to offer are loosed into my sons life now and it is exceedingly well with him.
AMEN.

27

DIVINE SELECTION

1 Peter 2:9
But ye are a chosen generation, a royal priesthood, an holy nation, a peculiar people, that ye should shew forth the praises of him who hath called you out of darkness into his marvellous light. (KJV)

MY DECREE

My son is always set apart by his exemplary behaviour. His conduct is constantly positive wherever he goes and he is a positive influence to others. He attracts friends of good character and behaviour and he is a role model to his generation.

MY PRAYER

Father, you have crowned my son and ordained him to succeed and prosper in all things (Psalm 8:5). Thank you that he is outstanding during every stage of his development: as a toddler, a child, a teenager, a youth, a young adult, father, husband, and in all areas that you have ordained in his life. Thank you that you keep him as the apple of your eye at all times.
AMEN.

BRAVERY AND STRENGTH

2 Samuel 23:8-39
Such were the exploits of the three mighty warriors ... There were thirty-seven in all. (NIV paraphrased)

MY DECREE

My son is brave enough to face every situation. The anointing for bravery that was upon David, Abishai, Ithai and all of David's men (described in 2 Samuel 23) is upon my son, by faith.
With God's help my son can scale a wall and advance against a troop (Psalm 18:29). He does not wilt when challenges come but with divine strength and resolve, he rises to every challenge. Like the Biblical Gideon, my son is empowered to be a mighty man of valour.

MY PRAYER

Dear Father, I thank you that my son is valiant and victorious at all times, regardless of the situation. He rises above challenges and temptations and is subduing every negative experience that comes his way. Thank you that with your help and according to Psalm 18:29, he can subdue obstacles, cross barriers and overcome anything that often stops other young men from attaining their God-given destinies.
AMEN.

29

ELEVATION

Habakkuk 3:19
The Lord God is my strength, and he will make my feet like hinds' feet, and he will make me to walk upon mine high places. (KJV)

MY DECREE

My son is mentally, spiritually, emotionally and physically buoyant. He has the divine ability to bounce back from any and all setbacks. As his parents, we are always financially able to provide for his education, extracurricular activities and all else that he requires. His spiritual needs are ministered to and he enjoys all-round blessing.

MY PRAYER

Dear Lord, thank you that in you, my son is strong and valiant. Thank you that by the cross, the blood and the name of Jesus Christ, he is elevated. By your grace, he reaches great heights and always makes it to the top. This is his heritage and inheritance in Christ.
AMEN.

EASE

Matthew 11:29-30
Take my yoke upon you, and learn from me; for I am meek and lowly in heart, and ye shall find rest for your souls. For my yoke is easy and my burden is light. (KJV)

MY DECREE

My son takes on only the weight of
Jesus Christ that is light and the yoke of Christ that is easy. Every burden that the Lord allows into my son's life is turned into a blessing. All things work together for my son's perfect good.

MY PRAYER

Abba Father, I thank you that you have good plans for my son, to prosper and not to harm him (Jeremiah 29:11). Thank you that he is confident enough to cast all of his burdens on you because you are faithful enough to give him rest whenever he needs it. By your love, his shoulders are free and never weighed down by life.
AMEN.

31

TRIUMPH

Micah 2:13
The one who breaks open will come up before them;
They will break out, Pass through the gate, And go out by it;
Their kings will pass before them, With the **LORD** at their head. (NKJV)

MY DECREE

Now and in the future, my son breaks through every barrier in his way. He breaks forth and breaks out. By the grace of God, my son overcomes every academic, emotional, spiritual, physical, mental, psychological and physiological hindrance in his way. My son dismantles all other obstacles to success in the name of Jesus Christ.

MY PRAYER

Dear Lord, thank you that you always go ahead of my son at every stage of his life. Thank you that all gateways to a better life are open to my son at all times. Anything that is not of your glory that seeks my sons life, his time, his mental and physical health and his destiny meets with you first. Thank you that you go before him and through his trust and confidence in you, you guarantee his victory.
AMEN.

HONESTY

Proverbs 11:1
A false balance is an abomination to the LORD, but a just weight is his delight. (ESV)

MY DECREE

My son is honest and true at all times. He achieves a perfect equilibrium of excellence in all areas of his life. His distinction evenly equalised across the board. His attitude, behaviour and character are well-tempered. My son maintains a healthy equanimity between work, play, recreation, entertainment, spirituality and in all facets of his life.

MY PRAYER

Dear Lord, Thank you that my son finds all aspects and facets of his life in you. Thank you that you give him divine strategies, methodologies and plans that are well aligned with your Word. Thank you that through you he is achieving multiple accolades at the same time. Nothing you have given him will slip through his life.
AMEN.

33

SALVATION

Romans 10:9
For if thou shalt confess with thy mouth the Lord Jesus, and shalt believe in thine heart that God has raised Him from the dead, thou shalt be saved. (KJV)

MY DECREE

The gift of salvation is freely given to my son. His spirit hosts the Lord and his spiritual eyes and ears see and hear the Lord in unforgettable ways. My son is spiritually available to the Lord and by way of divine and supernatural encounters, my sons physical life produces phenomenal results. My sons academics, relationships, finances and endeavours are all redeemed and safeguarded at all times.

MY PRAYER

Dear Lord,
Thank you that my son has received salvation through the liberating work of the cross of calvary, the redemptive power of the blood of Jesus Christ and the supremacy of the name of Jesus Christ. This salvation is guaranteed and nothing can pluck my son out of your hand (John 10:28) or remove the engravement of my sons name from the palm of your hand (Isaiah 49:15).
AMEN.

34

DAILY IMPROVEMENT

Proverbs 4:18
But the path of the righteous is as the shining light, that shineth more and more unto the perfect day. (KJV)

MY DECREE

Every area of my sons life keeps improving daily. He makes steady progress on a daily, weekly, monthly, termly and yearly basis. My son lives out a better life and relationship with Christ than I. He goes from better to best at every stage of his development. His spiritual and physical achievements are better than those of his parents and peers.

MY PRAYER

Dear Lord, Thank you that you are the light of the world and that he who finds you finds the light of life. Thank you that your light in my sons life illuminates and brightens all his experiences. Thank you that he is the light of the world - his light can never be dimmed (Matthew 5:14-16). Every darkness that approaches is unable to comprehend the light in him and due to your light, it retreats.
AMEN.

35

PREDESTINATION

Romans 8:28
And we know that all things work together for good to those who love God, to those who are called according to His purpose. (KJV)

MY DECREE

Only the best of everything comes into my sons life. Whatever is positively outstanding academically, emotionally, spiritually, physically and in all angles of life manifests in him now. His friends, teachers and his experiences are extraordinarily better than the rest. My son's opportunities are first-rate and he enjoys the utmost that life has to offer. He gives of his best at all times and strives to maintain a level of excellence in all areas of his life. The

MY PRAYER

Dear Lord,
Thank you that you have overcome the world and so I do not fear. I thank you that all the positive and negative things that my son has been through all combine to show him favour. Thank you that you are glorified by every experience in his life.
AMEN.

36

ENABLEMENT

Psalm 34:8
Taste and see that the LORD is good; blessed is the one who takes refuge in him. (NIV)

MY DECREE

My son is blessed: empowered to prosper and enabled to succeed and excel. He is fortunate in all things and at all times. He is favoured at night and during the day, at sundown, twilight and at dawn. Advantages and benefits follow him throughout the watches of the day. His mind, body, soul and spirit are always prosperous. He is an empowerment to me, my family and the world around him.

MY PRAYER

Dear Lord, thank you that all that is good and perfect comes from you. Thank you that you know all that I need before we ask for it. Thank you that you daily load my son and I with benefits (Psalm 68:19). I am grateful that in you we can find the blessing that makes my life rich and adds no sorrow (Proverbs 10:22). I claim this in the name of Jesus Christ.
AMEN.

37

HONOUR

Psalm 111:1 and 3
I will extol the Lord with all my heart…His work is honourable and glorious, and His righteousness endures forever. (KJV)

MY DECREE

My son is a positive reflection of his maker. My son is a vessel of honour and this is reflected in his attitude, behaviour, character and work at all times. My son is a blessing. The glory of the Lord has risen upon him and he is shining brilliantly. The Lord radiates on my son and this attracts good people and opportunities to him.

MY PRAYER

Dear Lord Jesus Christ, thank you that my son is made in your image and likeness. He has part of the wisdom and intelligence of the all-knowing and all wise God. Moreover, through Christ, my son not only has a sound mind (1 Timothy 1:7) but the mind of Christ (1 Corinthians 2:16). It is exceedingly well with him.
AMEN.

MEEKNESS

Psalm 32:8
I will instruct thee and teach thee in the way which thou shalt go; I will guide thee with mine eye. (KJV)

MY DECREE

Everything about my son's life is used to build him up in Christ. It works together and takes him to his divine destiny. His character is improving and growing better daily. God is moulding my son to fit into the unique place in life that God has predestined for him. My son is positively reinforced by everyone around him so that in turn, he raises all those around him. By grace, the Lord helps my son to construct and live out a better life than mine.

MY PRAYER

Our Lord and Saviour,
I thank you that your spirit is near enough to teach my son (John 14:26) and to increase his level of peace and clarity during his studies. Thank you that the promised holy spirit is teaching my son all things and through these teachings, my son is excelling. In the name of Jesus Christ, AMEN.

39

CONFIDENCE

Proverbs 3:26
For the Lord will be your confidence And will keep your foot from being caught. (NKJV)

MY DECREE

My son is brimming with a healthy and positive sense of confidence that comes from God alone. I am certain that my son shall testify of the Lords goodness in the land of the living (Psalm 27:13). The self-assuredness that was upon the Biblical David is also upon my son. My son finds strength in quietness and confidence, according to the Word of the Lord. The Lord empowers my son throughout his youth and beyond (Jeremiah 17:7).

MY PRAYER

Dear Lord,
Thank you that my son has a strong belief and faith in you and your abilities. I am grateful that through your spirit, these prayers and your words, He is fully trusting in you. Thank you that and all your promises are all "yes and AMEN." (2 Corinthians 1:20).
AMEN.

FOCUS

Proverbs 4:20-27
My son ... Give careful thought to the paths for your feet and be steadfast in all your ways. Do not turn to the right or the left; keep your foot from evil. (NIV)

MY DECREE

Just like God concentrated on creating life, my son focuses on and pays attention to the important things in his life. He does not veer away from the paths of righteousness (Psalm 23:3). The Lord shows him the path of life (Psalm 16:11). My son focuses on all areas of his life that bring about his development and betterment. By the grace of God, this emphasis leads to many good rewards. He does not walk with or listen to the ungodly.

MY PRAYER

Dear Lord, I thank you that my son is focusing on his lessons, inside and out of the classroom, lecture room and training centre. He is giving full attention to what he is taught, with interest. By divine empowerment, he is mentally sustaining that focus, strengthening his understanding and applying the information that he is assimilating. Thank you for this blessed hope.
AMEN.

COMFORT

Psalm 71:21
You shalt increase my greatness, and comfort me on every side.
(NKJV)

MY DECREE

The God of all comfort comforts my son whenever he is in need. As a result, my son becomes a source of consolation. My son is contended with the person God created him to be. Moreover, the word of God and the Holy Spirit are sources of constant reinforcement to my son. My son does not remain in a negative comfort zone. Instead, he is empowered by God to constantly renew his mind and achieve excellence.

MY PRAYER

Dear Lord, thank you that my son, like Gideon, is a man of valour by faith, regardless of what he thinks of himself in his low moments. He is growing and expanding exponentially in all things and on all sides. My son's vision, territory, gifts, and talents are expanding as he grows older. God's great destiny over my son's life and His purpose are realised and the influence of the Lord upon my son is great.
AMEN.

POWER

Ephesians 3:20
Now to him who is able to do far more abundantly than all that we ask or think, according to the power at work within us…
(NIV)

MY DECREE

My son is capable of greatness and uncommon achievement. Every hidden and untapped potential in him is revealed to the world. His aptitudes are endless. He is understanding and retaining all he is taught and he is skilled to the point of all round excellence. My son learns from every mistake and negative experience and keeps on improving.

MY PRAYER

Dear Lord, Thank you that my son has an innate ability and power to do all things through Christ, who gives him the strength that he needs. There is a great force of good that is exerted over my son's life, and it radiates through his thoughts, habits, speech, character, and ambitions. His life is powered by the work of the Holy Spirit, and he is doing well in all things.
AMEN.

43

DILIGENCE

2 Timothy 2:15
Be diligent to present yourself to God as one approved, a worker who does not need to be ashamed and who correctly handles the word of truth. (NIV)

MY DECREE

My son receives his abilities directly from God. He is capable enough and is receiving recognition and reward. His abilities are nurtured, developed, and revealed to the world. He acquires and cultivates advanced skills and competencies from a young age. My son is an all-rounder who has received a grace for excellence.

MY PRAYER

Dear Lord, I praise you because my son is making history in his generation. He has an excellent work ethic. He is moulded and shaped by the word of the Lord. Thank you that although he is young, the calling and potential on his life is great. I pray that many - young and old – will gracefully gravitate towards him to learn better ways of thinking and doing. Thank you for the spirit of God that manifests in wisdom inside of my son (Isaiah 11:2).
AMEN.

FREEDOM

Isaiah 49:25
But this is what the Lord says: "Yes, captives will be taken from warriors, and plunder retrieved from the fierce: I will contend with those who contend with you, and your children I will save (NKJV)

MY DECREE

The Lord fights with everything that battles with my son and his academic, physical, emotional, spiritual life and potential. With the help of the Holy Spirit and the might of the Lord, my son has the power of an overcomer and he is combating every challenge until it is overcome.

MY PRAYER

Dear Heavenly Father, I worship you because my son is kept safe and rescued by you at all times. Thank you that even though weapons may be formed against him, they will not prosper (Isaiah 54:17) and he will always be delivered from harm's way. Thank you for your protection over his mind, body, soul, spirit and property.
AMEN.

NETWORKS

Psalm 24:1
The Earth is the LORD's and everything in it, the world and all who live in it. (NIV)

MY DECREE

My son is connected to the Lord Jesus Christ who is his divine source of power and might. He is relating with with good friends and taking advantage of amazing opportunities. He makes special and favourable associations with all those who need to help him to realise his potential. All negative connections to anything or anyone evil currently or in the future are severed immediately. My son is inseparable from greatness, favour, divine protection, and provision.

MY PRAYER

Our Father, I praise you because although the devil is the prince of this world and the air, You are God and king over all the earth. The whole earth is filled with your glory. I thank you that you are able to orchestrate everything in my sons life and his experiences in accordance with your will (Ephesians 1:11). Thank you that your will is always to prosper and not to harm my son. Thank you that through your grace over his life, my son is benefitting from all your goodness and the riches of your glory in the Earth, in Christ Jesus.
AMEN.

HELP

Psalm 121:1
My help comes from the Lord, Who made heaven and earth
(NKJV)

MY DECREE

The assistance of the Lord, the heavenly hosts and angelic ministers is available to my son at all times. Through this aid, my son is making the best decisions for his life. He is supported throughout his education and character development. Kings, queens and princes provide succour to my son.

MY PRAYER

Dear Jesus Christ, I am in awe of you because you are my son's guide through life. You make things easier and possible for him. You divinely provide the right helpers who take him to the next level of his development. Thank you that your spirit is leading him and connecting him with the helpers he needs and disconnecting him from those who are not for his good. Thank you that with your help, my son achieves unimaginable things.
AMEN.

47

GREATNESS

Deuteronomy 6:18
And you shall do what is right and good in the sight of the Lord, that it may go well with you, and that you may go in and take possession of the good land that the Lord swore to give to your fathers. (NKJV)

MY DECREE

My son has an ever positive attitude. He responds well to positive correction and criticism and learns from it every time. He overcomes anything negative that befalls him. Through this attitude, he goes forth and prospers. His behaviour and character are constantly improving.

MY PRAYER

Dear Lord Jesus Christ,
I am confident that by your grace, I am raising a son who is upright and well able to take advantage of all the opportunities that you offer him. I trust in the fact that you correct, lead and guide him in the way he should go. You help him not to make costly mistakes and not to repeat those that I as his parent have made, and through you, he is living the better life that you have ordained for him even before he was born.
AMEN.

FULFILMENT

Philippians 1:6
Being confident of this, that he who began a good work in you will carry it on to completion until the day of Christ Jesus.
(NKJV)

MY DECREE

My son is achieving optimum development at every stage in his growth process. He is developing physically, spiritually, emotionally and academically. His trajectory is always upward and forward. He is confident, responsible, able and full of stamina. The Lord gives my son wisdom, transgenerational ideas and insights about whitty inventions (Proverbs 8:12) and he is creative and innovative. He develops resilience and tenacity, a positive attitude and new ways of good thinking.

MY PRAYER

Our Father, I thank you that everything and everyone you have made is good. All that is good and perfect comes from you. Through every experience that my son goes through, whether good or bad, I know and accept that you are working behind the scenes to carry out your good and perfect plan for his life. Thank you that nothing takes you by surprise. In your sovereignty, you anticipated every step that my son will take in this life and you have ordained it to be successful, regardless of how things may appear.
AMEN.

49

GOD'S PERFECTION

Psalm 138:8
The Lord will perfect that which concerns me; Your mercy, O LORD, endures forever; (NKJV)

MY DECREE

The Lord Jesus Christ fosters a sense of drive, vision and momentum in my son. Therefore, my son accomplishes great things in his generation. He lives positively and comes up with innovative ideas and inventions that benefit our family and his generation.

MY PRAYER

Our Father, you are a purpose driven creator. Thank you that you have made divine provision for my son to complete every challenge and task you have set for him in order for you to accomplish your will in his life. Thank you that he will live out and walk out your purpose for his life at every stage of his development. Thank you that even though on his way he may meet challenges , your peace and purpose always guide him. According to your word, you are perfecting all things concerning him (Psalm 138:8) and making his way perfect (Psalm 18:32).
AMEN.

50

DELIVERANCE

Matthew 6:13
...deliver us from the evil one. (KJV)

MY DECREE

The Lord rescues my son from evil. The Lord is the deliverer of my son whenever he is in trouble or when he does not know what to do. Supernatural assistance, aid and help is always at hand from my son even before he needs it.

MY PRAYER

Our Lord and Great Deliverer,
Thank you that for as long as you sit on your throne of greatness, no evil will succeed in the life of my son or in my life. No matter what traps may be set for my son in his life now and in the future, you have already made a way of escape and protection for him and for me. Thank you for delivering his academics, his character, his youth, his mind and self-esteem from every evil plan to thwart or delay his destiny. This I pray in the name of Jesus Christ.
AMEN.

BENEVOLENCE

Galatians 6:9
And let us not be weary in well doing good: for in due season we shall reap, if we faint not. (KJV)

MY DECREE

By the help of the Lord, my son applies diligence to all he does. This causes him to sit before kings and not unknown men. He works consistently and strategically and his efforts are noticed and rewarded. My son always applies himself and goes the extra mile to achieve great things.

MY PRAYER

Our Father,
I am grateful to you that my son is paying attention to all he needs to do in order to succeed. Thank you that he is consistent and always takes care to do his best at all times. Thank you that this effort will yield best results and will lead to success at all stages of his development.
AMEN.

FAITH

Hebrews 11:6
Without faith it is impossible to please God…(NIV)

MY DECREE

By the grace of our Lord Jesus Christ, all the positive expectations that I have about my son are being exceeded. In fact, He will do far much more than I can imagine. The great power of God is inside of my son and it is at work inside of all of his circumstances, at all times. This power achieves greater things than I, with my limited mind can grasp.

MY PRAYER

Heavenly Father, I thank you for this son that you have given me. Like Hannah, I hand him over to you so you (1 Samuel 1:28). You make all things beautiful so I am confident that you have even ordained things that I cannot dream of. You take him to places I cannot see and he achieves greater things than have ever come to our minds. Thank you that your power is limitless, you are omni-potent and he is made in your image and likeness. Thank you Lord for this young man and your role in his life.
AMEN.

53

ACADEMIC TEACHABILITY

Luke 6:40
A disciple is not above his teacher, but everyone when he is fully trained will be like his teacher. (NKJV)

MY DECREE

By the grace of the Lord, my son has been given an extraordinary ability and enablement to achieve academic success. My son is keen to learn about all positive things inside and outside of the classroom, on online platforms and in lecture halls. My son is always enthusiastic about life in general. He is even excited and ecstatic about the Lord and His love.

MY PRAYER

Our Lord and Saviour,
You alone are helping my son to transform his mind to walk out these confessions I am making. You alone are giving him the kind of desires that he should plant in his heart. Thank you that by faith, you help him to develop the kinds of ambitions, goals and steps he will need to make these declarations a reality in his academics and other areas of his life.
AMEN.

GRACE

2 Corinthians 9:8
And God is able to make all grace abound to you, that ye, always having all sufficiency in all things, may abound in every good work…(KJV)

MY DECREE

Our loving God crowns my efforts and those of my son with success. He exceeds all expectations regarding all his abilities. This is his portion at all times and in all things – regardless of challenges and circumstances. My son never runs dry but he is ever buoyant and productive, fruitful and ever-green. He is always relevant and he has the capacity to keep receiving and pouring out good things.

MY PRAYER

Dear Lord,
I thank you that your light will shine on everything I decree and declare and that it will come to pass. Thank you that I am a king, priests (Revelations 1:6) and ministers of your covenant written on my heart. Thank you that the word of a king is supreme and indisputable and that I shall eat the fruits of not just my words, but your Word regarding my son. You alone are our portion (Psalm 16:5). Therefore, all that I have dared to ask for, you will provide. I thank you for your consistent love and blessings to my family.
AMEN.

55

STRENGTH

Daniel 11:32
...but the people who know their God shall be strong, and do exploits. (KJV)

MY DECREE

The true nature of God is revealed to my son. With this knowledge, my son is doing the unthinkable in his generation. He shall not be taken advantage of but he seizes and benefits from every good opportunity that comes his way. He is a pioneer and makes positive history and in all things. According to his predestination in the plans of the Lord, he excels beyond anyone's wildest dreams. Generations young and old are favoured because of him.

MY PRAYER

Dear Lord Jesus Christ,
Your spirit is omnipresent, omniscient and omnipotent. You have given us part of it and baptised us in the promised holy spirit who serves as our counsellor, comforter and guide at all times. Thank you that through you and the power that my son received from the Holy Spirit when he believed and from the cross of calvary, he is always prospering in all that he does.
AMEN.

ANOINTING

1 John 2:27
But the anointing that you received from him abides in you, and you have no need that anyone should teach you. But as his anointing teaches you about everything, and is true, and is no lie - just as it has taught you, abide in him. (KJV)

MY DECREE

God has granted my son a grace for excellence in all that he does. The Lord has given my son a winning strategy for success. My son stands out positively in everything, including in the grace of giving. He works as though he is working for the Lord. My son excels in knowledge and speech. He is a positive example to all. Above all, he thinks about all that is excellent, admirable and praise worthy regarding himself and others.

MY PRAYER

Dear Lord,
Thank you that you have empowered my son to excel and exceed all expectations. You have enabled him to do great things in his generation and to be ahead at all times. Through the unique gifts and talent's you have packaged in him, he is able to naturally, simply and easily that which is required by the world around him.
AMEN.

57

PLANS

Proverbs 16:3
Commit to the Lord whatever you do, and the Lord will establish your plans. (NIV)

MY DECREE

All aspects of my son's life align to fulfil the plan of God for him. All elements of life and godliness work together to raise up and bless my son in all areas of his life. Every experience my son goes through is harnessed and oriented to achieve Gods purpose for his life. Everything that the enemy has intended for evil in my sons life is turned to good by the Lord.

MY PRAYER

Dear Lord,
I commit my sons life and education into your hands. I ask that you continue to lead and guide us and his teachers on how best he can realise, manifest and release his potential. I commit all of our plans for his education and life in general to you and have faith that you will establish them in accordance with your purpose for him.
AMEN.

LIGHT

Matthew 5:16
Let your light so shine before men, that they may see your good works, and glorify your Father in heaven. (KJV)

MY DECREE

My son makes exceptional improvements in all areas of his life. His good nature has a positive impact on those around him. His exceptional talents are recognised and nurtured everywhere and by everyone wherever he goes. He has an exceptional sense of focus and achieves much at each level of his development.

MY PRAYER

Our Father,
I thank you that you are the light of life (John 8:12).
Thank you for shining your light upon my son's life and his way. I need your light on my way as I lead him. I humbly ask that you would be my help in raising my son and realising his potential.
AMEN.

59

INTELLIGENCE

Proverbs 1:7
The fear of the Lord is the beginning of knowledge, But fools despise wisdom and instruction. (KJV)

MY DECREE

My son is open and receptive to opportunities to learn and excel at all times. His mind is porous to new and positive ideas about life. He approaches positive prospects with heightened interest and he enjoys the process of gaining favourable information from all walks of life.

MY PRAYER

Lord,
I thank you that my son is worthy of your love and attention. Thank you that the spirit of counsel, knowledge and wisdom is available to him through the holy spirit. Thank you that he comes into the knowledge of the holy spirit, the spirit of might, the fear of the Lord (Isaiah 11:1). I am grateful that wisdom characterises the decisions that my son makes at every important phase of his life.
AMEN.

60

FORWARD PLANNING

Proverbs 21:5
Good planning and hard work lead to prosperity, but hasty shortcuts lead to poverty. (ESV)

MY DECREE

By the grace of the Lord Jesus Christ, my son organises his affairs in a way that brings forth positive results in his life. He works in a smart and strategic way and this brings him good rewards. With ease, my son affords and pays the price for advancement.

MY PRAYER

Our Lord and our Father,
I seek your help in bringing out the best for my son in his education, life and future. I ask that your will be done and that you lead me in the way that I should go. With your help I can train him up in the way you have predetermined for him to go (Proverbs 22:6). I pray for the patience to make decisions that produce lasting results that are pleasing to you. I pray that my son will also receive the same grace to make wise decisions that establish him firmly in your good plans for his life.
AMEN.

61

HUMILITY

James 4:10
Humble yourselves in the sight of the Lord, and He will lift you up. (KJV)

MY DECREE

My son is respectful, courteous, modest, polite and successful. He is good to me and the people he meets. He gets along well with other people and is a pleasure to be around, regardless of his achievements. As parents, we are full of pride over the attitude, behaviour and character of my son at all times.

MY PRAYER

Dear Lord Jesus Christ,
I thank you for the grace to be a better person with an ever-improving attitude, behaviour, character and relationships with my son and others. Thank you that lift and elevate me in esteem and I achieve my higher calling as parent. I pray that you will replicate this in my son and give him a grace for humility.
AMEN.

62

ALERTNESS

1 Thessalonians 5:6
So then, let us not be like others, who are asleep, but let us be alert and sober. (KJV)

MY DECREE

My son is sober minded at all times. Nothing contaminates his mind and spirit. He is made in the image of God and no imagination that is contrary to the word of God over his life will stand. He is overcoming peer pressure to be worldly and vice-full. His thoughts about himself and others are wholesome and good at all times. No weapon formed against his mind will prosper.

MY PRAYER

Our gracious Lord,
Thank you that my son is enthusiastic, exuberant and pays full attention to educational and life lessons. Thank you that he is empowered and enabled by the spirit of God to channel his focus to what he is taught and to process it with the mind of Christ that you have given him (1 Corinthians 2:16).
AMEN.

63

ATTENTION

Job 32:8
But there is a spirit in man, And the breath of the Almighty gives him understanding.

MY DECREE

By the grace of the Lord Jesus Christ, my son is understanding all things that require his attention. By this insight, my son is blessed in all of his ways. He is achieving his God-given and predestined purpose in life and he does this early.

MY PRAYER

Lord Jesus Christ,
I thank you for the intellectual and emotional strength you have given my son. Thank you that the mind of Christ is at work in him and his achievements at every stage are praiseworthy.
AMEN.

64

GODLY PASSION

Romans 12:11
Never be lacking in zeal, but keep your spiritual fervour, serving the Lord. (NIV)

MY DECREE

My son is always enthusiastic about life, responsibility and learning. His eagerness is infectious to those around him. His abilities, skills and competencies are being nurtured and they are thriving. My son is equally interested and committed to developing a personal and ever-deepening relationship with Christ.

MY PRAYER

Dear Lord,
Thank you that by faith, my son is alert and consistent in producing work that is pleasing. He is enjoying his educational experiences and excelling at everything he is being taught. He is making steady progress and is on a forward moving trajectory through Christ who strengthens him.
AMEN.

65

SOCIAL STANDING

Titus 2:7-8
Show yourself in all respects to be a model of good works, and in your teaching show integrity, dignity and sound speech that cannot be condemned, so that an opponent may be put to shame, having nothing evil to say about us. (ESV)

MY DECREE

Good reports abound about my son's behaviour and comportment at all times. With an advanced sense of maturity, my son is leading his peers in all things. He is ever happy, caring, enthusiastic, joyful, prepared, focused, ready, equipped, blessed, excelling, smiling, and healthy. He is brimming with mental wealth and in top spiritual and physical form.

MY PRAYER

Dear Lord,
Thank you that my son is honest, upright, honourable, virtuous and sincere.
Thank you for empowering him to always do his best.
Thank you that he always displays decency, decorum, grace, morality and greatness.
Thank you that he is always praiseworthy, through the power that is in the name of our Lord, Jesus Christ.
AMEN.

INCREASE

1 Timothy 4:15
Give your complete attention to these matters. Throw yourself into your task so that everyone will see your progress. (NLT)

MY DECREE

My son emerges as a blessed and prosperous, successful and intelligent child of God. He manifests as a well-educated, upstanding, respectful, admirable and well-mannered young man. He develops into a responsible father, husband and son who does his best to uphold family and positive values. He rises as a leader and at the right time, he rules in his community and in the world at large.

MY PRAYER

Dear Lord Jesus Christ,
Thank you that my son makes advancements in all that is good and profitable. He keeps on going deeper into all that is good and perfect and found in you. Thank you that he is forging ahead, gaining ground, making strides and headway. Thank you that he can do all this through Christ who gives him strength.
AMEN.

PERSEVERENCE

Colossians 3:23
Whatever you do, do it heartily, as to the Lord and not men, knowing that form the Lord you will receive the reward of inheritance; for you serve the Lord Christ. (NKJV)

MY DECREE

My son always puts his best efforts forward. By the help of the Lord, my son is doing what is required of him at every point in his life. By the empowerment of the Lord, my son is organising himself and doing more than is required of him at every level. My son's efforts are fruitful and he is rewarded with positive outputs for the work that he has put in.

MY PRAYER

Dear Lord,
Thank you for empowering and enabling my son to achieve much through your spirit. By your grace, I ask you to empower him to always be industrious, productive and to work in a way that is pleasing. I ask that you provide him with the motivation to perform with excellence in all he does, as though he is working for your approval.
AMEN.

LIBERTY

Galatians 5:1
Stand fast therefore in the liberty by which Christ has made us free, and do not be entangled again with a yoke of bondage.
(NKJV)

MY DECREE

My son has been set free by Christ and he is free indeed. My son is liberated enough to be the person that God created him to be. He is has the resilience to learn, thrive, develop and excel. He is unburdened, unshackled and unhindered. He has the latitude that allows him to make the most of every experience. Out of this autonomy comes a noticeable sense of inner confidence that is expressed outwardly.

MY PRAYER

Dear Lord,
Thank you that you bought me freedom so that I can live in peace and believe in your Word. Thank you that you have given my son the privilege, right and power to live a life of empowerment. Thank you that my son works in a smart way that maximises productivity and condenses the time required to accomplish tasks. I pray that my son will not need to struggle, toil and slave for results but may they come with ease and the blessing of the Lord.
AMEN.

PROGRESS

Psalm 92:13
They are planted in the house of the Lord, they flourish in the courts of God. (ESV)

Ezekiel 47:12
And on the banks, on both sides of the rives, there will grow all kinds of trees for food. Their leaves will not wither, nor will their fruit fail, but they will bear fresh fruit every month, because the water flows from the sanctuary. Their food will be for healing and their leaves for healing. (ESV)

MY DECREE

My son flourishes at all stages of his life. Like a palm tree in the house of the Lord, he grows stronger at every stage. He prospers in all areas of his life. His path is growing proverbially brighter every day whilst his proverbial leaves continue to blossom and bear good fruit.

MY PRAYER

Dear Lord,
Thank you that my son's heritage in you is to grow and improve continuously. Thank you that he will continue to grow stronger and be better at all he does. Thank you that as his parent, I will also keep rising to every occasion and I will continuously be more than equal to the task. Thank you that we are a fruitful family whose roots are in the living waters of Christ and who leaves and fruit never wither but are ever green and full of life.
AMEN.

GODLY DESTINY

> **Ephesians 1:11**
> In Him we were also chosen, having been predestined according to the plan of who works out everything in conformity with the purpose of his will. (NIV)

MY DECREE

My son is predestined for greatness. He grows in favour, wisdom and stature. He stands out and is singled out for benefit and blessing. Man and God alike promote my son. Extraordinary opportunities line up for him because of the advantage that the Lord has bestowed upon my son.

MY PRAYER

Dear Lord,
Thank you that my son is called by you and marked for good things that come from and through you. I ask that you continue to develop and highlight his positive attributes so that they attract uncommon opportunities that he will exploit with your help. Thank you that you empower and enable him in an uncommon way to achieve and accomplish unusual things in his generation.
AMEN.

71

PRAISE WORTHINESS

Luke 5:26
Then everyone was astounded, and they were giving glory to God. And they were filled with awe and said: We have seen incredible things today." (CSB)

MY DECREE

My son lives a life filled with accomplishment, achievement, accolades, awards, amazing experiences and all things blessed. My son rises exponentially in all areas of his life. He gains a positive reputation in all he does. His trajectory is stratospheric.

MY PRAYER

Dear Father,
Thank you that you are faithful and I can depend on you to bless my son with a good life. Thank you that your presence in his life is so evident that many marvel at the person he is and the things he is achieving with ease. Thank you that all these things are possible because I believe in you and your power and according to our faith it shall be unto us.
AMEN.

BELIEF

2 Corinthians 5:7
For we walk by faith, not by sight. (KJV)

Hebrews 11:1
Now faith is the substance of things hoped for, the evidence of things not seen. (KJV)

MY DECREE

Through a strong belief in himself and in the Lord, my son creates history and new heights for others coming behind him to emulate. By faith and good works, my son is positively exceptional. My son outperforms expectations and excels in all areas of life. The Holy Spirit helps my son to be pleasing to God because his faith is coupled with good works. My son will live a long and good life.

MY PRAYER

Dear Lord,
Thank you that my son is pleasing you at every step of his life, by his faith. Thank you that faith comes to him through hearing the word of God and that through your favour, you give him ever greater measures of faith to build on. Thank you that you are the author and finisher of his faith and that you use the faith you have given him to shape his life in accordance with your will.
AMEN.

73

FAVOUR

Proverbs 3:4
So shalt thou find favour and good understanding in the sight of God and man. (KJV)

MY DECREE

Because of the Lord's favour, my son finds his purpose and destiny at a young age. He understands the keys of life and the things of the Lord. He finds favour with all that matter to his future and they open gates and doors of opportunity for him. He finds the path to life and its illumination grows brighter and brighter and brighter daily (Proverbs 4:18).

MY PRAYER

Thank you Lord,
that my son has a good name, a good reputation and an elevated status in the eyes of all that know his name. Thank you that every negative word spoken to, of, or about him bears no fruit and that it is replaced with your word for him, in all areas of his life.
AMEN.

74

CELEBRATION

Isaiah 55:12 For you shall go out with joy, And be led forth with peace: the mountains and hills shall break forth into singing before you, And all the trees of the field will clap their hands.
(KJV)

MY DECREE

By the grace of the Lord, there is celebration around my son's life and achievements. Peace, organisation, power, good pleasure and joy colour his life and experiences. He is a pleasure to be with and around. He is turning every mundane experience into something enjoyable and colourful.

MY PRAYER

Most gracious Lord,
Thank you that this world and this life, this generation and those to come will show my son favour. Thank you that his life is worth living and that it is filled with strategic open doors and opportunities and relationships that will help his destiny to manifest. Thank you that all of this will work in conformity with your will to ensure that my son is successful in all areas of his life.
AMEN.

75

GOD'S PRESENCE

1 Samuel 18:14 In everything he did he had great success, because the Lord was with him. (NIV)

MY DECREE

Through the blessing of the Lord, my son achieves great things in life. He is far from mediocrity, evil, harm, sickness, disease, calamity, accidents, sudden disasters and premature death. Mischief and laziness, defeat and demotivation, depression and lack of self-belief and anything that is not of the Lord's glory remains far away from my son. In their place, the Lord gives my son all he needs for empowerment and success.

MY PRAYER

Thank you Lord that my son is near to you and your house always. Thank you that he is close to godly friends who are helping him to walk out his God-given destiny.
May he always be close to us as his parents and may good things always be within his reach.
AMEN.

76

GOD'S FAITHFULNESS

Isaiah 46:4
Even to your old age, I am He, And even grey hairs, I will carry you! I have made and I bear; Even I will carry you, and will deliver you. (NKJV)

MY DECREE

By the mercy and providence of the Lord Jesus Christ, my son lives out all the years ordained for him by the Father. The flame of life that God placed in my son's life does not dim or be blown out too soon. All those around him fan into flame the gifts that God has placed in my son and he performs well in all things as a result. He excels throughout every day the Lord has ordained for him (Psalm 139:16).

MY PRAYER

Thank you Lord, that the life that you have given my son is profitable – it benefits current and future generations. Thank you that my son always finds his life within you and in your courts, meditating upon your statutes and precepts. I pray that with you as His provider, my son never lacks any good thing. Thank you that at every challenging and difficult point of his life, he knows your presence and that you will be there for him and that he will always find his life in you.
AMEN.

77

STATURE

Colossians 1:10
That ye might walk worthy of the Lord unto all pleasing, being fruitful in every good work, and increasing in the knowledge of God. (KJV)

MY DECREE

By the help of the holy spirit, my son's efforts always bear good fruit. He produces bumper harvests of positive results. My son is identified by his pleasing works.
He constantly exhibits the fruits of the Holy Spirit which are peace, love, gentleness, goodness, kindness, patience, joy, faithfulness and self-control (Galatians 5:22).

MY PRAYER

Dear Lord,
Thank you for your grace and mercy in my son's life. Thank you that he will continually be fruitful in all areas of his life. Thank you that he will come to know you more and more at every stage so that he can grow in the knowledge of God.
AMEN.

78

ACADEMIC FOCUS

Proverbs 4:25 Let your eyes look directly forward and your gaze be straight before you. (NIV)

MY DECREE

By the help of the Lord, my son diligently focuses on his work. He concentrates on what he is meant to be learning. His concentration does not shift but it is squarely and solely on what he is instructed to do. My son only pays attention to what is positive about life and his learning experience.

MY PRAYER

Dear Lord,
Thank you that my son is focused: he concentrates and pays attention to the things that you have set before him. I pray that he will always look to you and not remove his gaze from the things of God, at all times and phases of his life. May you bestow upon him the ability to have laser type of focus that achieves good results in all areas of his life.
AMEN.

ALTITUDE

Psalm 18:35
You give me your shield of victory, and your right hand sustains me; you stoop down to make me great. (NASB)

MY DECREE

The Lord stoops down to make my son great (Psalm 18:35). The progress made by my son is evidence of the Lord's presence in his life. He receives an exceedingly great reward for all his efforts. My son's attitude is good and his advancement is commendable. His interactions, experiences and relationships are positive and he experiences great peace and progress at every stage.

MY PRAYER

Dear Lord Jesus,
I thank you that you have already surrounded my son with protection, you have guarded and placed a defence around him. Thank you that he has success, he is triumphant and victorious in all he does. Thank you that your presence is with him and that you make him significant, prominent, distinguished and important in all he is involved in.
AMEN.

80

BRILLIANCE

John 8:12
Again, Jesus spoke to them, saying, "I am the light of the world. Whoever follows me will not walk in darkness, but will have the light of life" (NIV)

MY DECREE

My son lives in a realm of brilliant light that shines through and around him. It defends him and ushers him into the company of other people of light. My son has received every spiritual gift necessary for success in his education and in life. The Lord has gifted him with grace and mercy from God and man. All hidden gifts and talents are uncovered and they serve my son and the world at large well.

MY PRAYER

Dear Father,
Thank you that you are light, you are faithful and that your steadfastness surrounds my son at all times. Thank you that you remain a constant help and presence in his life. Thank you that my son grows to depend on you, your reliability and your light that beams ahead and all around him. Thank you for being a dependable and ever-present force in his life.
AMEN.

SOUNDNESS OF MIND

2 Timothy 1:7
For God hath not given us a spirit of fear, but of power and of love, and of a sound mind. (KJV)

MY DECREE

My son is courageous; he makes valiant efforts and functions to the best of his cognitive ability and beyond. My son is not nervous or timid: his gallantry shows in all he does. He is encouraged, motivated, keen and enthusiastic. The peace and presence of the Lord in his life leads him to have positive mental well-being, courage and strength.

MY PRAYER

Dear Lord,
I thank you that any fear or trauma that ever entered my sons life is transformed into resilience and conquering power. Every door opened by those experiences is shut, never to reopen. Through your grace, my son is powerful beyond measure and there is a Godly force that is mightily at work in him. Thank you Lord for giving him a grace for self-control, self-restraint and self-mastery for the good of your kingdom.
AMEN.

82

GIFTEDNESS

James 1:17
Every good gift and every perfect gift is from above, coming down from the Father of lights, with whom there is no variation or shadow due to change. (ESV)

MY DECREE

The Lord has given my son gifts and callings that are a blessing to him, us and the world in general. My son is stable in mind, spirit and character. The only changes he makes are for his betterment and that of others. This establishes him in good works. My son is the light of the world and an endowment to it. His light shines consistently through all he does.

MY PRAYER

Dear Jesus Christ,
Thank you that all that is good and perfect comes from you. Thank you that You perfect all things concerning my son (Psalm 138:8). Thank you that you light up all facets of his life and cause his experiences to be positive. Thank you that your light constantly shines brightly in his life at all times, through all ages and stages and into eternity.
AMEN.

83

STEADFASTNESS

Jeremiah 17:8
He is like a tree planted by the water, that send its roots by the stream, and does not fear when the heat comes, for its leaves remain green, and is not anxious in the year of drought, for it does cease to bear fruit. (ESV)

MY DECREE

The Lord leads my son to green pastures of fruitfulness and peace. My son is surrounded by nourishment and fruitfulness, freshness and life. The leaves from his tree of life are evergreen because he is like a tree planted by the river of living water. They do not wither but bear fruit in season. He is surrounded by good, positive and godly friends who know and seek the Lord (Psalm 1:1).

MY PRAYER

Dear Lord Jesus Christ,
Thank you that you alone are the firm spiritual foundation
of my sons life (1 Corinthians 3:11).
I thank you that his roots are found deep inside of you.
I ask that in all seasons and at all times, my sons life will be fruitful, fertile, bountiful and ever abounding. I ask that he will be ever relevant and buoyant, strong and powerful at all times.
AMEN.

84

NOBILITY

Psalm 10:16
The Lord is king forever and ever (KJV)

MY DECREE

The Lord Jesus Christ is king of all kings. He is a sovereign king maker. He presides over my son and every seed of nobility and royalty that has been placed in him. The Lord is king forever and he anoints my son with a sacrament for greatness and the ability to preside over all areas of his life at all times.

MY PRAYER

Dear Father,
Thank you that you are Lord of lords, the King of the earth and that you are the ultimate father to my son. Thank you for your lordship over his life and the potential that you have placed in him. His greatness will manifest in his generation and beyond. By faith, he will do greater things than those who came before him through your great power.
AMEN.

85

PROMOTION

Isaiah 60:17
Instead of bronze, I will bring you gold, and silver in place of iron. Instead of wood I will bring you bronze and iron in place of stones. I will make peace your governor and well-being your ruler. (NIV)

MY DECREE

My son always strives for the gold medal in all areas of his life. He receives promotion at every stage and level. His behaviour, conduct, character and attitude are consistently being improved and upgraded. He is anointed to succeed incrementally and exponentially.

MY PRAYER

Dear Lord,
Thank you that even in times of trouble in his generation, my son will experience a better life than those around him. Thank you that you will always raise the standard for him. May he always be elevated at every level and amongst all his peers. May peace, righteousness and excellence always guard him and be evident in all areas of his life.
AMEN.

EMINENCE

Psalm 18:33
He makes my feet like the feet of a deer, And sets me on high places. (NKJV)

MY DECREE

The mighty hand of the Lord lifts up my son and he reaches great heights in life. Blessing, accomplishment and honour are his heritage. He reaches the pinnacle of his predestination.
He is always being uplifted: mentally, emotionally, spiritually and in his soul. This translates into positive results all round.

MY PRAYER

Dear Father,
Thank you that at every level, you are training my son to go higher at every phase of his life. May he forever be peaking, achieving and summiting higher. Thank you that his attitude, behaviour and character sustain him in high places.
AMEN.

87

REVELATION

Psalm 119:130
The entrance of thy words gives light; it giveth understanding unto the simple. (KJV)

MY DECREE

By the speaking out of these very words, the illumination that is in the word of the Lord is bringing light into and around my son.
It is visible in every phase of his life. Understanding, elucidation, revelation and light radiate in my sons world. He is finding his way easily at all times.

MY PRAYER

Father,
Thank you that my son will always bring luminescence wherever he goes. Through your word, may he light up dark places and may darkness retreat because of the power of Your word in his life.
AMEN.

GRATIFICATION

Psalm 4:7
You have put gladness in my heart… (NKJV)

MY DECREE

My son is joyous and he rejoices in everyday that God has granted him. My son is happy at school, amongst his friends and in the community. At home, he relates well with his family. He makes me glad and I am proud of him.

MY PRAYER

Dear Father,
I pray that you continually anoint my son with the oil of gladness of heart. May he be the source of delight to your people. May he be fruitful and potent in all areas of his life. As his parents, may we always be pleased with his progress.
AMEN.

89

MOMENTUM

Psalm 92:12-14
The righteous flourish like a palm tree, they will grow like a cedar of Lebanon. Those that be planted in the houses of the Lord shall flourish in the courts of our God. They will still bring fruit in old age, they shall be fat and flourishing (KJV)

MY DECREE

My son is flourishing. He is growing in the Lord and in the power of his might. His attitude and character improve daily. He is daily increasing in mental and spiritual knowledge, intelligence and understanding. He is developing into a man of honour and stature. He grows more confident, more intelligent, more forthright, more obedient, and more pleasurable. He always lives with more blessing and accomplishment.

MY PRAYER

Father,
I pray that my son will be found in the church and positive company throughout his youth and beyond. May he abound and thrive in your presence even until his old age. May he always have time and opportunity to fellowship with others and to rightly divide the word of God with those around him.
AMEN.

RESILIENCE

Isaiah 41:10
...I am your God. I will strengthen you, Yes I will help you; I will uphold you with My righteous right hand. (NKJV)

MY DECREE

By God's grace, my son possesses the strength, resilience and power that he needs to navigate life. Whenever he is down, the Lord raises him up and supports him. There is no end to the height of his potential and the love of God for him. The Lord elevates my son to a place of glory in this life.

MY PRAYER

Dear Lord Jesus Christ,
Thank you that in times of need, you will be with my son in a visible and tangible way. Thank you that you will send him assistance and aid whenever it is needed, at the right time and through the right means. I pray that he too will be help to others in their time of need.
AMEN.

91

UPRIGHTNESS

Proverbs 23:24
The father of a righteous child has great joy, a man who fathers a wise son will rejoice in him. (NIV)

MY DECREE

My family and I are always blessed with the perpetual progress that my son is making. Through the love of God, the blessing and gift of wisdom is at work inside of my son. He makes wise decisions that are pleasing and he will live long. By God's grace, the Holy Spirit manifests as wisdom in my son's life (Isaiah 11:1).

MY PRAYER

Lord Jesus Christ,
I pray that you will continually grant wisdom to my son. May he be wise beyond his years at every stage. May that wisdom be matched with understanding of the world and the things of your Kingdom.
May he make wise decisions that are led by the Holy Spirit. May you lead me in the way that I should go about raising a son as unique as him.
AMEN.

HONESTY

3 John 1:4
I have no greater joy than to hear that my children are walking in truth. (KJV)

MY DECREE

My son is set free by the truth of the Lord over his life. The belt of truth is fastened around his waist (Ephesians 6:14). This truth pushes and propels my son further and he arrives at his place of pre-ordained purpose at every key stage. My son does not entertain or believe the lies of the enemy because the devil is a liar and the father of lies and his native language is lies (John 8:44) and my son knows this.

MY PRAYER

Father,
I pray for my son to always follow your leading. I pray for him to perpetually accept your truth about him and his destiny. Please give him revelation, knowledge and understanding of your truth about life. May all of his questions be answered and may his faith in you be established for life and generations to come.
AMEN.

93

HEALTH

Jeremiah 33:6
…I will bring health and healing … I will heal my people and will let them enjoy abundant peace and security. (NIV)

MY DECREE

My son lives in a realm of radiant health. He is healed at all times. The Spirit of God is in him to regenerate every physical, mental or spiritual aspect of his life. Every part of my sons life is perpetually healthy. Most importantly, he enjoys not just mental health but mental wealth.

MY PRAYER

Dear Lord,
I pray that my son prospers in his soul so that he can be brimming with all-encompassing health. May he be disciplined in the way he looks after and feeds his body, mind and soul. Grant him emotional health and heal all soul wounds. Give him a cheerful heart so that he can be healthy. May he enjoy peace and security of the mind, soul, body and emotions.
AMEN.

SKILL

Exodus 31:3-11
I have filled him with the Spirit of God, with wisdom, with understanding, with knowledge and with all kinds of skills ...
(NIV)

MY DECLARATION

The Lord grants to my son a special grace for superior skills and excellence. Many look up to my son and follow him because he is a leading example in terms of character, work and conduct, at all times. My son is a leader who is sought after for his rare skills and favoured by all he meets.

MY PRAYER

Dear Father,
I pray that you would anoint my son with your Spirit, with wisdom, with understanding, with knowledge and with all kinds of abilities. I pray that you will pour the anointing and empowerment to be skilful upon my son at all the stages of his life. May that God-given skill raise his profile and seat him with other skilled people.
AMEN.

95

BENEDICTION

Numbers 6:24-25
The LORD bless you and keep you; the LORD make his face to shine on you and be gracious to you; the LORD turn his face toward you and give your peace. (NIV)

MY DECREE

The face of the Lord is perpetually turned to my son. The glory of the Lord radiates over his life. The light of the Lord within my son leads him in prosperous paths. The Lord empowers and enables him to prosper in all areas of life. Christ is the light of life and in that light, my son finds and fulfils his destiny. He is taught by the Lord and his peace is great.

MY PRAYER

Dear Lord,
Thank you for your presence in the life of my son and your influence over every area of his life. Thank you that you empower him to prosper at all times and that this is his God-given heritage. May your countenance not be turned away from him but may you radiate your life giving light upon him and may it shine through him to the world around him.
AMEN.

96

GRACEFULNESS

John 1:16
Out of his fulness we have all received grace in place of grace already given. (NIV)

MY DECREE

By grace, my son's academic abilities manifest in his life and the world around him. Every confession and positive word spoken here is realised and actualised immediately. Hard work, diligence, excellence, effort, understanding and a genuine love for learning manifest in my sons life now and in the future. At every stage, my son remains in control and he is overcoming any challenge that besets him. He is surrounded by the grace of God.

MY PRAYER

Father,
Thank you for your love for my son and the generations that are to come. Thank you for the unmerited favour you have placed upon his life. I ask that you continue to bestow upon him, the grace for excellence, patience, skill and for all the good things that he requires for life and godliness. Thank you that you are adding to the grace that is abounding in all areas of his life.
AMEN.

97

INSIGHT

Proverbs 2:6
For the Lord gives wisdom, from his mouth cometh knowledge and understanding. (KJV)

MY DECREE

My son is mentally astute and intelligent. The right people are on hand to cultivate his brilliance in ways that I cannot presently think, ask or imagine. My son's natural and innate acumen helps him to excel and to make intelligent decisions. The enlightenment of God resides in my son and it is the spirit and breath of God that is within him that gives him understanding (Job 32:8).

MY PRAYER

Dear Lord,
Thank you that the Holy Spirit manifests in my son as the spirit of wisdom, understanding and knowledge. Thank you that my son will continually get understanding and revelation of the deep things of the Lord at all times.
AMEN.

VIRTUE

Proverbs 2:9
...you will understand righteousness and justice, equity and every good path. (KJV)

MY DECREE

The Holy Spirit operates in my son and gives him the right level of intuition needed at every point. By this help, my son makes the right choices and brings to remembrance all the profitable things that he has been taught. He chooses the right friends and makes the best life decisions. This wisdom grows with his age, sets him apart and enables him to accomplish great things in life.

MY PRAYER

Dear Lord,
Thank you that you teach my son how to love justice. I am confident that you will continuously bestow upon him that which is good, just and right. May he always act with equity, objectivity, justice, fairness, honesty and righteousness. Through your power and favour, your mercy and grace, my son is walking in your paths of justice and righteousness.
AMEN.

99

DOMINION

Psalm 22:28
For the kingdom is the LORD's, And he rules over the nations.
(NKJV)

MY DECREE

By virtue of the cross of calvary, my son is part of the kingdom of God. My son has accepted the gift of salvation. It is visible and tangible in all that my son does. It is because of the kingdom that my son consistently performs well at all stages. He takes advantage of global opportunities. My son is influential across all nations and he is a blessing to his generation.

MY PRAYER

Dear Lord,
May your kingdom come into my sons life. Thank you that you rule over all men and the nations and you have given my son jurisdiction over a purpose-oriented territory on earth. Thank you that your glory covers the earth and that the weight of this glory covers all areas of my sons life. I ask that you command favour for my son from all the nations and peoples that your rule and that you will subdue nations under him (Psalm 18:47).
AMEN.

100

ENJOYMENT

Ecclesiastes 2:24
There is nothing better for a man, than that he should eat and drink, and he should make his soul enjoy good in his labour. This also, I saw, was from the hand of God. (KJV)

MY DECREE

My sons life is characterised by good rewards and access to open gates, doors and windows of opportunity. He works wisely and effectively with the joy of the Lord at all times. The world around him is blessed with the excellent work of his hands.

MY PRAYER

Dear Lord,
By your grace and favour, I am grateful that my son lives a life in which he strikes a perfect balance between work and good leisure. I pray that he will partake of the blessing of the Lord that makes rich and adds no sorrow (Proverbs 10:22). May he do great things with ease and accomplish much at every phase of his life.
By faith in Christ I pray.
AMEN.

101

SECURITY

Psalm 5:11
But let all who take refuge in you be glad; let them ever sing for joy. Spread your protection over them, that those who love your name may rejoice in you. (NIV)

MY DECREE

My son's life is hidden in Christ (Colossians 3:3) and he is kept by the Lord. He therefore radiate the joy that comes from being in the presence of the Lord. This joy is then converted into his strength (Nehemiah 8:10). With this strength, my son is exceling as a diligent and smart-worker. He is reaping good success which in turn brings him gladness.

MY PRAYER

Dear Lord Jesus Christ,
Thank you for being the deliverer and shelter of my son. Thank you that you are his shield and buckler and his ever present help at all times. Thank you that you protect and shield him and that he is in a joyful relationship with you. Thank you Lord that my sons happiness, pleasure, delight and elation will always be visible and tangible at all times. May he always draw on the power inside your name so as to overcome challenges at every phase of his life.
AMEN.

102

EFFORT

Colossians 3:23
Whatever you do, work at it with all your heart, as working for the Lord, not for human masters. (NIV)

MY DECREE

My son is committed to always applying the best of his efforts and abilities to all he does. He is always keen to learn and improve. He always strives for excellence. He does not work in vain but receives a righteous reward for his labour.

MY PRAYER

Dear Lord,
Thank you that all that is good and perfect comes from you. Thank you that diligence, consistency, steadfastness, effort and all that my son needs in order to excel in his studies, work and endeavours have been found in you.
Thank you that by relying on your spirit that empowers and brings understanding, he will excel in his work. Thank you that he is close enough to you, and that he takes pleasure from working in a way that pleases you.
AMEN.

103

DIVINITY

1 Peter 2:9
But you are a chosen people, a royal priesthood, a holy nation, Gods special possession, that you may declare the praises of him who called you out of darkness into his wonderful light.
(NIV)

MY DECREE

Because of his salvation, my son is a child of the Lord who is the King of kings. According to this word of God, my son is a king himself. As biblical royalty, my son has an inheritance of kingship that is upon him wherever he goes. As such, he always inspires the best in and amongst his peers. Everything in his life works together to honour him and he is in good standing with the Lord.

MY PRAYER

Dear Heavenly Father,
Thank you for creating my son in your image and after your own likeness. Thank you for selecting, appointing, anointing and consecrating my son for kingship and priesthood (1 Peter 2:9).
Thank you that his appointment by you is irrevocable because you do not go back on your word. Thank you that you have given him everything that he needs in order to accomplish your purpose for his life. By faith, I declare that all of his endeavours and relationships continually bring out the best in him.
AMEN.

104

FRIENDSHIPS

Proverbs 18:24
There are "friends" who destroy each other, but a real friend sticks closer than a brother. (NLT)

MY DECREE

My son finds good, upright and positive friends at all stages in life. He associates exclusively with people of good character and comportment. He gravitates towards and meets with other positive individuals who are also drawn to him. They spur him on and bring out the best in him. By God's grace, my son is always part of a thriving ecosystem that is achieving great things.

MY PRAYER

Dear Lord Jesus,
You are the closest and most faithful friend to me and my son. By faith, I declare that my son will always be aware of your companionship and closeness and that his life will be guided by it. Thank you that it is this friendship that will attract other godly people who are taught by you, into his life. I thank you that his path will not meet with that of bad influencers. Instead he will be friends with people who are also your friends so that his bond with you will always be strengthened.
AMEN.

105

DIVINE LOVE

1 John 4:19
We love him, because he first loved us. (KJV)

MY DECREE

The Lord loves my son and my son loves God. This devotion is reflected in his work and all areas of my son's life. In turn, everyone around my son works together to ensure that his great destiny is fulfilled on, and ahead of time. The love of God leads and guides my son in all he does and his relationships, including with himself.

MY PRAYER

Dear Lord Jesus Christ,
Thank you that you love the soul of my son. Thank you that you predestined, chose, called and loved him before any of us knew that he would exist. Thank you that your love preserves him in all of his ways and that as a loving father, you have prepared only good things for him in all areas of his life. I am confident that this love will accomplish many extraordinary things in his life. I pray that he will come to the fullest knowledge of how much you love him.
AMEN.

106

DIVINE KNOWLEDGE

Isaiah 54:13
All thy children shall be taught of the Lord; and great will be the peace of thy children. (KJV)

MY DECREE

The Lord is a teacher to my son. By the help of the Lord, my son is acquiring the knowledge, skills and experiences that are relevant to his future. I am also taught the best way to communicate with and bring out the best in my son. Everyone involved in my sons life is understanding his gifts and talents and gains the wisdom regarding how to turn any weaknesses into strengths.

MY PRAYER

Dear Lord Jesus,
Thank you for your word. Thank you that you have exalted it above your name (Psalm 138:2). Thank you for promising us that the fruit of our womb is blessed (Deuteronomy 28:4). Thank you that you defend these promises for your names' sake. Thank you that you keep every vow you have made to us in your word: that you are not a man that you should lie and you do not repent of your word (Numbers 23:19).
AMEN.

107

ASCENDANCY

Daniel 2:21
He controls the course of world events; he removes kings and sets up other kings. He gives wisdom to the wise and knowledge to the scholars. (NLT)

MY DECREE

Through the power of God's hand, my son rises above all limitations. The support of the Lord brings promotion and lifts my son above all obstacles. The hand of the Lord bestows upon my son: wisdom, power, ability, strength, success and academic achievement. It causes him to rise above all of his circumstances.

MY PRAYER

Our gracious Lord,
I thank you for your promises over the life of my son. Thank you for your hand that is not too short to reach my son (Isaiah 59:1). Thank you that you hold his life and times in your hands and that you have ordained all of his days before he lives them out. Therefore you know when he will need to be lifted up. Thank you that by your hand, my son is standing on great heights and his brilliance is visible to the world around him, including good people who are blessing him.
AMEN.

108

ADVANTAGE

1 Chronicles 4:10
Oh Lord that you would bless me indeed and enlarge my territory! Let your hand be with me, and keep from harm so that I will be free of pain. (NIV)

MY DECREE

By the grace and favour of the Lord, all negativity in my son's life is turned around. His physical and spiritual territory is blessed with prosperity. By the mercy of the Lord Jesus Christ, my son is blessed with success, peace of mind and the mind of Christ. My son is part of a peculiar people with an uncommon and extraordinary calling on his life. The potential of my son is recognised, realised and released for the benefit of the world around him.

MY PRAYER

Our loving Father,
I thank you that my son is a blessing to us and those around him. Thank you that you enable and empower him to prosper at every stage and in all areas of life. Thank you that according to your word, you have already glorified him and given him everything he needs, pertaining to life and godliness (2 Peter 1:3).
Thank you that you have given my son a large and positive sphere of influence and that he is touching and changing many lives. By faith, I declare that you are protecting all areas of his life.
AMEN.

109

COMPLIANCE

Proverbs 16:20
Whoever gives heed to instruction prospers, and blessed is the one who trusts in the Lord. (NIV)

MY DECREE

By God's grace, my son is perceptive and discerning . He always takes heed of teachings and lessons about life. His friends, teachers, coaches, parents and the Lord our God listen to him when he expresses his needs and makes contributions. My son has spiritual ears to hear and he listens to positive instruction and as he lives out these teachings, he is successful.

MY PRAYER

Dear Lord Jesus,
By faith, I thank you that my son is meek and humble and that he has a teachable spirit. Thank you that he is taking directives with humility. Thank you that this is reflected in his academics and all areas of his life. By faith I declare that he takes heed of lessons about life and godliness and that his heart conforms to your word.
AMEN.

110

INTEGRITY

Proverbs 4:18
But the path of the righteous is like the morning sun, shining ever brighter till the full light of day. (NIV)

MY DECREE

Christ is the light of my son's life. The light of the word of God shines on every way that my son takes. My son is the salt of the earth and his light is glowing in the dark wherever he goes. The light of God that is in everyone and everything shines and is
reflected on my son.

MY PRAYER

Dear Lord Jesus Christ,
I am grateful that you have given me a son that is kind-hearted, good, morally upright and decent. Thank you that he has accepted the gift of salvation and that he qualifies for a life that is brilliant, ever improving and abundant. All forms of anger, depression, unresolved hurts, bitterness, trauma and other dark experiences will never withstand the light that you are, combined with the light that he is and the light that I am. Darkness has no place in my son's life.
AMEN.

GODLINESS

Psalm 1:1
Oh, the joys of those who do not follow the advice of the wicked, or stand around with sinners, or join in with mockers. But they delight in the law of the LORD, meditating on it day and night. They are like trees planted along the riverbank, bearing fruit each season. Their leaves never wither, and they prosper in all they do. (NLT)

MY DECLARATION

The life of my son is rooted in Christ who is the living water. My son therefore never thirsts. He walks with the righteous who always challenge him to stand firm in the Lord. His proverbial leaves are always ever-green and his branches are ever fruitful. No philosophy, teaching or instruction from the world will be overrule the word of God that is in my son. Praise for the Lord shall always be upon his lips.

MY PRAYER

Lord Jesus Christ, the giver and granter of abundant life, thank you that you constantly water my son with life and praise for you alone. Thank you that you have predestined my son and already caused all things to work together for his good. I am grateful that he walks with wise and upright company.

His counsel is always godly and you have anointed godly friends and relationships for him. Thank you Lord that my son flourishes academically and is spiritually feeding others good and pleasant spiritual food. I pray this by faith in your name.

AMEN.

112

ABUNDANT LIFE

John 10:10
The thief does not come except to steal, and to kill, and to destroy. I have come that they may have life, and that they may have it more abundantly. (NKJV)

MY DECLARATION

My son has been given everything he needs pertaining to life, godliness and success. By the grace of God, the intelligent life of the Lord is in my son's brain, body, mind, soul and spirit. By faith, every hidden talent, gift, skill, power, strength, agility, power and ability in my son is brought to life and light now.

MY PRAYER

Dear Lord, I thank you that you came for my son to live a life of superabundance in you. Thank you that this life force has been with him since conception and it will continue until all the days you have ordained for him on earth are complete. Thank you that from here onwards, the life of Christ continues to function in my son and in all of his affairs.
AMEN.

113

ORDINATION

1 John 2:27
But the anointing that you received from him abides in you, and you have no need that anyone should teach you; but as the same anointing teaches you concerning all things, and (it) is true, and (it) is not a lie, and just as it has taught you, you will abide in Him. (NKJV)

MY DECLARATION

My son is blessed and anointed by His maker. Through this consecration, my son is achieving greater things than his parents. Sanctified as he is, my son reaches great heights and his positive achievements are many.

MY PRAYER

Heavenly Father, I thank you that my son is anointed to prosper academically and in all areas of life. Thank you that this anointing is going to last throughout his entire life-time. May it continue to imbibe, revive and rejuvenate his understanding in all areas of life. This anointing causes my son to excel throughout his life.
AMEN.

MIGHT

2 Timothy 1:7
For God has not given us a spirit of fear, but of power and of love and of a sound mind. (NKJV)

MY DECREE

My son is strong in the Lord and in the power of his might. He is delivered from fear and it is replaced with great faith. My son is a mighty man of valour like Gideon in the Bible (Judges 6:12). Through the power of God, my son is performing well in all areas of his life.

MY PRAYER

Dear Lord, I thank you that the spirit of the Lord dwells within my son. I thank you that it manifests in the form of self-control and a sound mind. Thank you that by your Spirit, my son makes good decisions, his behaviour is upright and his attitude is godly attitude.
AMEN.

115

PROSPERITY

Jeremiah 29:11
For I know the plans I have for you, plans to prosper you and not to harm you, plans to give you a hope and a future. (NIV)

MY DECREE

By His grace, God is making all good things flourish in the life of my son. Through Christ my son is progressing, advancing, doing well and thriving in all areas of his life. By the power of the Lord Jesus Christ, all circumstances and people in my son's life combine to bring him blessing, opportunity and success.

MY PRAYER

Dear Lord, I thank you that my son lives out the plans that you have for him at every stage. Thank you for your goodness, grace, mercy and favour over his life. By faith, I thank you that I witness these blessings at work in my son at every stage.
Thank you that every day, every phase, every season of my son's life confirm the plans that you have pre-destined for him.
AMEN.

116

BRIGHTNESS

Matthew 5:16
Let your light so shine before men in such a way that they may see your good works and glorify your Father which is in heaven.
(KJV)

MY DECREE

My son is the light of the world. He is connected to Christ, the light of life. This light drives out all darkness and failure. It enables my son to perform to his maximum ability. The light of understanding elucidates every path on which my son walks and his way is bright and prosperous.

MY PRAYER

Our Father,
I thank you that the light of God is outshining and blinding all forms of darkness in my sons life, at every phase and stage of his growth and development. I thank you that the world around my son, his generation, our family and those coming behind him marvel at the display of the light of God in his life.
AMEN.

FORGIVENESS

1 Timothy 2:15
For there is one God, and one mediator also between God and man, the man Christ Jesus. (KJV)

MY DECREE

By the grace of the Lord, my son is flourishing in a life giving relationship with Christ Jesus. This union is the basis of a thriving bond that my son has with our God, the Father. This alliance mitigates, mediates and heals all other relationships and experience that my son is involved in. Where things have gone wrong, I am grateful that they are being corrected and turned into a blessing. Jesus Christ remains the centre of my son's relationships both now and all the days of his life.

MY PRAYER

Lord Jesus Christ,
I am grateful for the blood of Jesus Christ that reconciles my son to the Father and to us his parents. Thank you that you are my son's advocate (1 John 2:1) before the Father. Thank you that you are separating him from anything that is not of your glory and to detaching him from evil. Thank you for reconciling my son to your promises and your purposes.
AMEN.

118

REDEMPTION

Ephesians 1:13
And you also were included on Christ when you heard the message of truth, the gospel of your salvation. When you believed, you were marked in him with a seal, the promised Holy Spirit. (NIV)

MY DECLARATION

By the grace of the Lord Jesus Christ, my son is marked for greatness with the seal of the Holy Spirit. By faith, the spirit of God is cultivating and producing good fruits in my sons life, for others to enjoy. By the working of the holy spirit, my son's life is chosen for all encompassing success and he continues to improve and evolve daily.

MY PRAYER

Dear Lord Jesus Christ,
Thank you for the gift of the Holy Spirit. Thank you Holy Spirit for being my son's counsellor, helper and friend. Thank you that nothing can separate my son from the plans and purposes of the Lord for him. I pray that the Holy Spirit continues to lead and guide my son and the generations that are to come after him.
AMEN.

COUNSEL

Psalm 32:8
I will instruct you and teach you in the way you should go; I will counsel you with my loving eye on you. (NIV)

MY DECLARATION

By God's grace, my son is led by the spirit of the Lord in all that he does. He receives and follows divine direction and guidance regarding all aspects of his life.

My son is on an upward move in all other areas of his life. The Holy Spirit removes every obstacle, barrier or hindrance in order to make a way for my son to follow constantly. By the power of the Holy Spirit within my son, he is commanding every hindrance to move and it obeys him. He overcomes all obstacles, blockages, barriers and diversions that he finds along his way.

MY PRAYER

Dear Lord,
Thank you for all the lessons that you have taught and continue to teach my son. Thank you for the ways in which you have led him to this point and for where you are taking him.
Thank you that you are the inner teacher that he can rely on at all times.
Thank you that you continuously teach him how to walk in paths of righteousness.
AMEN.

120

TRANSFORMATION

Romans 12:2
Do not be conformed to this world, but be transformed by the renewal of your mind, that by testing you may discern what is the will of God, what is good and acceptable and perfect. (ESV)

MY DECLARATION

By the grace of God, my son has a sound mind of Christ and great success comes from his intellect. His mind makes judgments that are positive and it is constantly restored, revitalised, rejuvenated and repaired. My sons mind leads him to the place of the fulfilment of his God-given destiny. My son is always positively improving, recalibrating and refreshing his intellect with good and positive thoughts. His thinking functions to its maximum capacity and he feeds it with good thoughts. Every dark thought and imagination is flooded with light and it diminishes.

MY PRAYER

Dear Lord,
By faith, I decree and declare that my son possesses the mind of Christ. This mind teaches and leads him in all that he does. Therefore, he is positively assimilated into the world around him and makes the best decisions. I thank you that through Christ, my son is renewing his mind and to focus on your purposes for him.
AMEN.

121

MODEL BEHAVIOUR

1 Timothy 4:12
Don't let anyone look down on you because you are young, but set an example for the believers in speech, in conduct, in love, in faith in purity. (NIV)

MY DECLARATION

Through the love of God, mental, spiritual and academic maturity are evident in my son's life. My son takes an extra-ordinarily progressive stance to all areas of his life, at all stages. His words, deeds, attitudes, responses and actions are always advanced. My son is wise beyond his years.

MY PRAYER

Dear Lord Jesus Christ,
I ask that you separate my son from anything that seeks to influence him negatively. I ask that the angels that you have given charge over my son make sure that every facet of my sons life is impeccable at every stage. I ask that his peers and those around him will look up to him as a leader and someone who is positively outstanding in all his interactions.
AMEN.

122

PRESERVATION

John 10:9
I am the door. If anyone enters by Me, he will be saved and will go in and out and find pasture. (NKJV)

MY DECLARATION

Christ is the way to the Father and my son uses him as a navigator and compass throughout life. Through Jesus Christ, my son is prospering on his way to academic and all-round success. Christ leads my son to the still waters of peace and into the presence of God, the Father. My son is lead into pleasant places and to the places holding the hidden treasures of the earth.

MY PRAYER

Dear Lord Jesus Christ,
I thank you for the day on which my son took the step to believe with his heart and confess with his mouth that Jesus Christ is Lord. Thank you that that was the day on which he was saved and begun to live out the promise of abundant and eternal life.
In times of confusion, when he is going astray or when he is backslidden or going through a wilderness experience, you will lead him back to yourself. May he continue to enter into realms of blessing and perpetually enjoy safe, lush and abundant pasture.
AMEN.

SUPREMACY

Colossians 2:15
And having disarmed the powers and authorities, he made a public spectacle of them, triumphing over them by the cross.
(NIV)

MY DECREE

By the power vested in me by Jesus Christ, I declare that every force, authority, influence and energy that is not of God has no power over my sons life.
Every thought and feeling, imagination, idea, philosophy, mentality or anything else that is not of God or contrary to Gods word about my son was nailed to the cross of Jesus Christ. It has no place in my sons life.

MY PRAYER

Our Father,
I thank you that You are the Most High God.
Thank you that you are the ultimate authority over everything.
I thank you that Jesus Christ has been given the name above every name.
Thank you that He is above all powers, principalities, rulers and every high thing that exalts itself above the knowledge of God. Every power, no matter how strong will not work against my son. Thank you that my son's life is now hidden in Christ (Colossians 3:3) and an abundant life (John 10:10) is his heritage.
AMEN.

124

CHRIST MINDEDNESS

1 Corinthians 2:16
For who hath known the mind of the Lord, that he may instruct him? But we have the mind of Christ. (KJV)

MY DECREE

My son possesses the intellect, comportment and manner of Christ.
His intellect is powerful, agile, strong and pure at all times.
He is filled with wisdom, knowledge, understanding, good judgment, discernment, prudence and enlightenment.
His thoughts are stayed on the things of God.
Every angel given charge of my son comes to his aid expeditiously and immediately when he needs to recall concepts or perform anything at any time.

MY PRAYER

Dear Lord Jesus Christ,
Thank you that you have given my son your mind.
Thank you that through this intellect, he is achieving great things with ease.
This mind is withstanding whatever life throws at it.
Through this triumphant intelligence, my son lives a life of victory.
My son is living the life that Christ died for him to have.
AMEN.

125

PROTECTION

Hebrews 12:29
For our God is a consuming fire. (KJV)

MY DECREE

By God's grace, everything that does not represent His glory in my son's life is destroyed by the consuming fire of God. Every stronghold, imagination or high thing that exalts itself above the knowledge of God in my sons life is pulled down and destroyed (2 Corinthians 10:5).

MY PRAYER

Our Father,
thank you that you destroy anything that is not of your glory from my son's life. Thank you that you have the power to dissolve anything that is not of your glory in his life.
Thank you that the fire of your glory burns throughout my sons life at all times. Thank you that it is a purifying fire that protects and destroys everything that is not of God.
AMEN.

126

PEACEFULNESS

1 Corinthians 14:40
For God is a not the author of confusion but of peace…(KJV)

MY DECREE

My son's life is lived with a clear conscience in all things. His thoughts are orderly, positive and pleasing. He has mental and psychological, spiritual and emotional clarity about the goodness within him and the world he lives in. As a natural consequence of this, success flows out of everything that he does, wherever he is and at all times. My son is made in the image of God and his imaginations are godly.

MY PRAYER

Father, thank you that the peace of God that transcends all understanding guards my son's heart and mind in Christ Jesus.
Thank you that my son is calm and peaceful. He has clarity of mind and a confident outlook that is ever positive.
AMEN.

127

AUTHORITY

Jeremiah 1:9
Then the Lord put forth his hand, and touched my mouth. And the LORD said unto me, Behold, I have put my words in your mouth. (KJV)

MY DECREE

By God's grace and mercy, the lips of my son are anointed to speak good things over himself and the world around him.
My son is confident and speaks with authority, clarity, accuracy and command. He is extrapolating, explaining and exposing the word of God into daily life.
Knowledge, understanding and wisdom effortlessly flow out of his mouth. He speech is always positive, relevant and pleasant to the hearer.

MY PRAYER

Dear Lord Jesus Christ,
Thank you that my son talks in a way that glorifies you and the world around him.
Thank you that he is an anointed mouthpiece of peace and blessing. I also pray that those around him also express life-giving words that build him. May my son positively shape his life through powerful, life giving and prophetic words that you give to him.
AMEN.

PROVIDENCE

Romans 8:28
And we know that in all things God works for the good of those who love him, to them who are called according to his purpose.
(KJV)

MY DECREE

My son lives out Gods original purpose for his life. The Lord's plan for him is coming to pass. My son is enabled and empowered to achieve that which the Lord has pre-ordained for him. Every original blessing is coming into his life and I enjoy it.

MY PRAYER

Dear Lord Jesus Christ,
I thank you for every virtuous, excellent and worthy cause that you have predetermined and included in my sons life.
I am grateful that you have put measures into place to ensure that my son answers your call over his life, at every stage that the call is issued.
I thank you that he hears you and follows your lead as you guide him to his place where you have planned for him to be at all times.
AMEN.

129

LIBERATION

Philippians 4:13
I can do all things through Christ who gives me strength.
(NIV)

MY DECREE

By the grace of God, my son is brimming with positive energy. His trajectory is upward, he is blessed and highly favoured. He is achieving much more than he can ask, think or imagine and this is according to the power of God that is at work in him. I declare that he always lives with vitality, revitalisation, energy, force, abundance, zest, zeal and effervescence. These qualities enable him to accomplish much.

MY PRAYER

Dear Lord Jesus Christ,
Thank you that the life that you have given my son is enlivened inside of him. May his life be led by the Holy Spirit to thrive and flourish and be full of your provision, glory and power.
May your light surround him at all times and may he live out all the days that you have ordained for him in your books.
AMEN.

130

ORDINATION

Daniel 11:32
...but the people that do know their God shall do mighty exploits (KJV)

MY DECREE

I serve the Almighty God and through Him my son achieves the extraordinary. My son is not ordinary. He abilities and achievements are remarkable. His schooling experience is positively noteworthy and filled with a love of learning. All my sons learning activities are filled with life, energy, positivity and a can-do attitude.

MY PRAYER

Dear Lord Jesus Christ,
Thank you that my son is part of the elect that you have set apart for yourself and your glory (1 Peter 1:1). Thank you for all the things that you are achieving through him and those he is achieving through you. I pray that you will enable him to show forth your excellence in all of his ways and achieve immense ventures for his generation. I ask you to continually help him to display a noble character. May his unique abilities be manifested in his work and relationships and may his works be a reward to the world.
AMEN.

131

HIS INTELLECT

Proverbs 18:15
An intelligent heart acquires knowledge, and the ear of the wise seeks knowledge. (NIV)

MY DECREE

My son's mind is free to learn. The grace of the Lord opens doors to understanding, knowledge, wisdom and uncommon expertise to him. My son is open to new and positive learning experiences. God has set before him open portals of opportunity and academic success that no one can shut. My son is exposed to positive learning experiences and he masters them with an open mind. He gets understanding and it enables him to exploit positive opportunities and experiences.

MY PRAYER

Dear Lord Jesus Christ,
Thank you that you have given my son a heart that is perceptive and astute with a bright, sharp and attentive mind. Thank you that he has an uncommon awareness, understanding and comprehension of the ways to gain knowledge. Thank you for revealing the expertise that you have woven into his soul. May he walk in enlightenment, awareness and perception at all times and in all of his affairs.
AMEN.

132

GOOD RELATIONSHIPS

Colossians 4:5
Be wise in the way you act towards outsiders; make the most of the opportunity. (NIV)

MY DECREE

Through Gods mercy, my son exploits all opportunities to learn, lead, grow, develop and to move forward to his maximum potential. The Lord creates circumstances that ensure that my son is upgraded and enhanced by outsiders and the people he meets. His peers and all people in authority are using their skills and training to benefit my son and I am ever pleased with his progress.

MY PRAYER

Dear Lord Jesus Christ,
Thank you that you have aligned my son's life with uncommon possibilities. Grant him the ability to always perceive and make the most of them for the benefit of your kingdom and the world around him. May he take every opportunity to learn what is in his curricular, syllabi and revision programmes, job descriptions and all related material. May his judgment and intelligence be a blessing to those with whom he interacts. May he also be a teacher of many lessons to those he meets.
AMEN.

133

PROVIDENCE

Jeremiah 29:11
"For I know the plans I have for you" declares the Lord, "plans to prosper you and not to harm you, plans to give you hope and a future." (NIV)

MY DECREE

Through the good will of the Lord, my son lives out every pre-ordained plan that God has for him. My son is well aligned with the plans of the Lord, whatever sphere he find himself in, whether that be at school, university, in the work place or in the community. No plan or weapon formed against my son and his future succeeds, it does not work and ends in failure.

MY PRAYER

Dear Lord Jesus Christ,
Thank you that you have scheduled great things into my son's destiny. Empower his life to acknowledge and respond to them all on time. In your mercy, cause every arrangement you have predestined for his benefit to be manifested in all his affairs. By your grace and will, he does not miss any part of your plan for him but he lives out every intention that you have for him.
AMEN.

134

PRE-DETERMINATION

Job 42:2
I know that you can do all things; no purpose of yours can be thwarted. (NIV)

MY DECREE

My son has been predestined for greatness. He lives his God-given purpose at every stage and every phase of his life. Every goal and objective that the Lord has set for my son is achieved in time and on time. The intentions and aims of the Lord for him are accomplished.

MY PRAYER

Dear Lord Jesus Christ,
Thank you that you are the holder of all power and that by faith, you exercise it in favour of my son. By your mercy, no other objective, target, intent or plan that is contrary to your will prevails in his life. Thank you that your word about his life is final and that your sovereignty in his life cannot be challenged.
AMEN.

135

THOUGHTS

Philippians 4:8
Finally brothers and sisters, whatever is true, whatever is noble, whatever is right, whatever is pure, whatever is lovely, whatever is admirable – if anything is excellent pr praiseworthy - think about such things. (NIV)

MY DECREE

My son's mind is free of all evil imaginations. All dark thoughts are immersed in light and this brings victory to my son. He thinks wholesome thoughts that build him up from the inside. He is made in the likeness of God and his imaginations come from the Lord alone. The mind of Christ thinks through him at all times. Every negative thought is taken captive to Christ.

MY PRAYER

Dear Lord, thank you that you guide my son in all truths and that he is free from all negative thoughts and feelings that may arise inside of him. Thank you that he does not listen to any voice that is not yours and that he does not see visions that are not from you. Let his thoughts be aligned with your word inside him and your innate purposes for him.
AMEN.

136

HONOUR

Isaiah 60:11
Your gates will be open continually. They will not be closed day or night, so that men may bring to you wealth of the nations, with their kings led in triumphal procession.(NIV)

MY DECREE

By the grace of the Lord my son is led by the Holy Spirit into realms of blessing, empowerment to succeed and prosper. He is positioned at the right place and the right time to meet the right people. This leads him to success, wealth and the company of royalty and the key people that he needs to achieve Gods purpose for his life.

MY PRAYER

Dear Lord Jesus Christ,
Thank you that through the Holy Spirit, my son is respectable, he walks in integrity, honesty and virtue in all his endeavours. I ask that by your grace, he is inspiring and attracting esteem in all his interactions. I am confident that by your spirit, and by faith, his character and deportment attracts the best people to his life. Empower him to be a pleasure for his teachers and trainers to instruct so that excellence is reflected in his academic and work-based endeavours.
AMEN.

137

BEST RESULTS

Ephesians 3:20-21
Now to him who is able to do exceedingly, abundantly above all that we ask or think, according to the power that works in us, to Him be the glory in the church by Christ Jesus to all generations, forever and forever. (NIV)

MY DECREE

There is a power at work in my son and it brings him success in all areas of life. It is a godly and spiritual force, authority, capacity and potent ability that works in his circumstances. The Lord is surpassing all expectations in my sons life and I am pleasantly surprised by what the Lord has in store for him. My son always does better at all times and I am blessed by the achievements of the Lord in his life.

MY PRAYER

Dear Lord Jesus Christ,
Thank you that it is in your sovereign nature to always be perfect towards us. Thank you that through your grace I obtain favour that brings goodness and glory into our lives. Thank you that by faith, you are answering the prophetic prayer of thanksgiving I am making. For the divine energy, influence and authority of the holy spirit that is potently at work in us and my son, I thank you.
AMEN.

138

PROTECTION

Psalm 121:8
The Lord will guard your going out and your coming and going from this time forth and forever. (NIV)

MY DECREE

By his mercy, the Lord preserves my son's life at all times. My son's mind is protected, conserved and safeguarded by the power of God. The Lord maintains His spirit of understanding and instruction inside of my son. The Lord creates a system made up of divine wisdom, knowledge, understanding, enthusiasm, diligence and effort and it is sustained and functional in my son. Moreover, my son upholds and preserves every word of God and positive instruction given to him at home.

MY PRAYER

Dear Lord Jesus Christ,
Thank you that you keep, save, protect and secure my son in all of his ways. Thank you that you are his protector and his guardian. You are his stronghold, his high tower, his strong tower, his shield and shelter. Nothing shall by any means harm him. His feet and all of his ways are braced and armed by you and you guide them in paths of righteousness that shine brighter and brighter.
AMEN.

139

PRESERVATION

Psalm 121:7
The Lord will protect you from all evil; He shall preserve your soul. (NKJV)

MY DECREE

The Lord has given his angels charge over my son, to preserve, protect and safeguard him wherever he goes and in everything he does. No evil comes near my son or his dwelling place. The angels and the spirit of the Lord ensure that my son has everything that he needs to enjoy the best in life.

MY PRAYER

Dear Lord Jesus Christ,
Thank you that you always defend, guard, shelter and cover my son with your powerful love and protection. Your faithfulness provides a covering over him and your love surrounds him in all of his ways. No weapon formed against his academics, mind, body, soul or spirit or any area of his life can remove your shadow that surrounds him and for that blessed assurance, I am eternally grateful.
AMEN.

140

GOD'S PRESENCE

Psalm 148:1-4
Praise the Lord! Praise the Lord from the heavens; praise him in the heights! (NKJV)

MY DECREE

The Lord deserves all the glory, exaltation and honour for the great works that he is doing in the life of my son. We exalt the Lord because by His grace, the intelligence that is in my son finds expression and fulfilment in all areas of his life and decision making. My son realises, manifests and releases his potential to the world around him and it is a marvellous wonder to behold. He is ever buoyant and successful and this is because of the power of God that is at work in his life.

MY PRAYER

Dear Lord Jesus Christ,
I cherish and applaud all your works in the life of my son. Thank you that they cause us all to adore you and declare your greatness to all. May these praises lead to more praises that will lead us to venerate you more. May my son serve the Lord. I extol you for all you are doing in my son's academics, his attitude, his character and his behaviour. I pay tribute to the evidence of you love and providence in his academics. I exalt you for all that you continue to do for my son.
AMEN.

141

PRIDE WORTHINESS

Proverbs 23:25
May your father and mother rejoice: may she who gave birth to you be joyful! (NIV)

MY DECREE

My son is the pride of his parents, our entire family and his generation. He makes me proud and uplifts the name of our family. I am celebrating his accomplishments and achievements.
His life showcases the faithfulness, goodness and glory of God over our bloodline. My son thrives and prevails in all areas of life, surpassing every threshold of prosperity and he enters into the realm of positive fame. He advances and makes further inroads into places no one in our family has been before.

MY PRAYER

Dear Lord Jesus Christ,
Thank you that I celebrate the achievements of my son with gladness and jubilation because of your grace. Thank you that I am always cheerful and delighted by the evidence of your spirit in his life and in his academics. Thank you for all that he achieves through your power, at every stage of his life. I am perpetually glad to see evidence of your faithfulness and kindness towards him in his academics and all walks of his life.
AMEN.

142

CHARACTER

Ephesians 4:2
Be completely humble and gentle; be patient, bearing with one another in love. (NIV)

MY DECREE

By the grace of God, my son walks in humility, kindness and meekness. He has a teachable spirit. Through a process of quick and accurate self-discovery, he finds the area of life that he was born to excel in. With time, patience, exposure and positive support, he is moving seamlessly into his realm of brilliance. He exhibits tolerance, perseverance, calmness, self-control and restraint.

MY PRAYER

Dear Lord Jesus Christ,
In your name I express my faith that you will continuously build my son's character. I believe that it is your good pleasure to teach him meekness, modesty, humility and all things that build godly character. Your loving kindness is granting him peace, calmness of spirit and a benign nature. By enabling him to be tolerant and to forgive out of a clean heart, you give him a Christ-like nature. Thank you that through a grace for self-control you empower him to be well tempered, composed and restrained even in the most heated situations. Thank you that by your spirit, you empower him to subdue overcome every spirit of anger, bitterness, offence and hurt and to recover quickly from attack, injustice and negativity.
AMEN.

PIETY

2 Peter 1:3-4
His divine power has granted to us all things that pertain to life and godliness, through the knowledge of him who called us to his own glory and excellence, by which he has granted us to his precious and very great promises, so that through them that you may be partakers of divine nature.(ESV)

MY DECREE

By God's grace, my son He is made in the image of the Lord, his creator. This sacred nature is reflected in his work, attitude, behaviour, character, comportment and deportment. Like his maker, my son produces work of a superior quality at all times. He lives a clean, temperate and composed life that is upright and blessed. He walks in the intimate knowledge of who and whose he is and what he has been called to do.

MY PRAYER

Dear Lord, I ask that you will help my son to live a life that is well balanced with piety, devotion and devoutness to you. By your power, may he enjoy his life virtuously, always giving reverence to you. I am confident that your holy spirit empowers my son to be holy, just as you have created him to be. By your grace, his lifestyle is always tempered with the presence of your spirit that leads and guides him in all his decisions. You have given him a godly nature and I pray that this nature will govern his studies, his relationships, decisions and every part of his life.
AMEN.

DEFENCE

Psalm 5:12
Surely, Lord, you bless the righteous; you surround them with favour as with a shield. (NIV)

MY DECREE

The Lord supports and benefits my son, promoting, helping and encouraging him in countless ways. The Lord gives advantages, preference and endorsement to my son. By faith, this and every other year is the year of Gods favour over my son's life. As a result, my son is excelling in this year and growing exponentially, becoming better and improving in all he does. In this year, my son is applauded and he receives the aid needed for him to exceed all expectations, with ease.

MY PRAYER

My righteous and loving Father, I thank you that according to your immutable word, my son is the righteousness of God in Christ Jesus. He is upright, honourable, honest, ethical, decent, just, principled and right in all his ways. Other righteous people are attracted to him and he walks only with the wise and virtuous. By your love, you cover his life and academics with support, aid, courtesy and help when he needs it. Thank you for promoting him spiritually, emotionally and in his soul. Through your spirit, may he always meet with good turns and physical and spiritual assistance. May he live and move in a circle of your protection security, preservation and your defence.
AMEN.

145

GODLY ALIGNMENT

Luke 3:5
Every valley shall be filled, and every mountain and hill shall be brought low, and the crooked path shall be made straight, and the rough ways shall be made smooth. (KJV)

MY DECREE

By the grace of God, my son is elevated from any low place that he may be in. The hand of the Lord is uplifting my son and setting him on great heights. Every barrier and hindrance in my sons way is being removed by the Lord because of the cross of calvary. By the help of God, my son overcomes all obstacles that stand in front of him. The road ahead of my son is being evened-out by the Lord.

MY PRAYER

Jesus Christ thank you that you lead my son at all times. Thank you that through your presence, my son leaves dark places. Thank you that you are the way through which my son comes out of difficult places and into the presence and blessing of the Lord. Thank you that Jesus Christ is the light that leads my son, the bread of life that nourishes him and the living water that strengthens him to overcome challenges. Thank you that the holy spirit leads and guides my son in all truth and delivers him from any places that he may find himself in.
AMEN.

146

BENEVOLENCE

Ephesians 2:10
For we are His workmanship, created in Christ Jesus unto good works which God hath before ordained that we should walk in them. (KJV)

MY DECREE

By God's faithfulness, the real potential and identity of my son comes to light and life now. My son lives out the abundant life that God predestined for him before conception. My sons potential to succeed and excel is divinely nurtured and cultivated and it bears good fruit at every stage. He has the capacity to perform to the very maximum of his potential. My sons achievements are great and excellent, respectable and worthy and they are a blessing to his family and community.

MY PRAYER

Dear Lord Jesus Christ,
Thank you for knitting my son together within yourself so that he may show forth your excellent nature. Thank you that you have predetermined success in all of his academic and other endeavours. Thank you that you have prepared perfect works for him to accomplish and that by your grace and mercy we are seeing the evidence of this in all areas of his life.
AMEN.

147

VIRTUE

Deuteronomy 29:29
The secret things belong to the Lord our God, but those things which are revealed belong to us and to our children forever, that we may follow all the words of this law. (NIV)

MY DECREE

The holy spirit is given as a gift to my son. He manifests to my son as the spirit of revelation, knowledge, understanding, might, counsel and fear of the Lord. He dwells inside of my son and brings out best that is inside my son, for the world to enjoy. By the promise of the Lord, secret keys to success are shown to my son and he moves forward and upward by the help of the Lord.

MY PRAYER

Almighty God,
I pray that through your spirit of revelation you shed light on the mysteries of life to my son. May your spirit of understanding, that dwells in men reveal all that is required for my son to succeed.
I thank you for elucidating the paths that my son walks, through your word and grace. Thank you for empowering me to walk in revelation of the things that bring out your purposes for his life.
AMEN.

148

POTENCY

Psalm 144:12
May our sons flourish in their youth and be like well-nurtured plants. May our daughters be like graceful pillars, carved to beautify a palace. (NLT)

MY DECREE

My son thrives, blooms, progresses and does well in his youth. He spends his youth wisely as a stepping-stone for bigger and greater things in his future. To our delight his youth is spent for the Lord, accomplishing much. Even when he is older, his youth is always renewed at every stage. Being ever-youthful and wise, my son takes every spiritual territory that belongs to him.

MY PRAYER

Dear Lord Jesus Christ,
Thank you that my son is strong and buoyant, firm and strong, fruitful and productive, energetic and vibrant in every phase of life. Thank you that his trajectory is always upward and forward.
Thank you that my son is showing forth abundant life in all that he does and that he is ever fruitful, well-cultivated, and well nutrified in all areas of his mind, body, soul and spirit.
AMEN.

149

PRAISE FOR THE LORD

Deuteronomy 10:21
He is the one you praise; he is your God, who performed for you those great and awesome wonders you saw with your own eyes.
(NIV)

MY DECREE

My son gives acclaim to the Lord whom he glorifies consistently. My son applauds the Lord and brings honour to the kingdom of God. This is in response to the perfect works that the Lord is doing for my son. I am ever celebrating with my son because he continuously excels in all things. I appreciate the Lord because of all the accolades and achievements my son is obtaining.

MY PRAYER

Lord, I praise you. I glorify and laud you with honour and exaltation for all your wonderful works in my sons life. Thank you that you reign supreme over everything pertaining to his life and his godliness.
Thank you that you reflect your awesome glory throughout my sons life and that his life shows evidence of your love and providence.
AMEN.

150

DIVINE NATURE

Genesis 1:27
So God created mankind in his own image, in the image of God he created them; male and female he created them. (NIV)

MY DECREE

My son has been moulded, shaped and created to be like his creator. This means that he is powerful beyond measure and rules and reigns over the circumstances in his life. My son is celebrated as an individual and neither his race nor colour is taken into consideration against him at any time. He fulfils a unique purpose and excels in it without comparing himself with others or being distracted.

MY PRAYER

God, our Father in heaven, you are awesome and your works, including my son, are all marvellous.
You alone are excellent and I am amazed at your power in my son's life.
Thank you that you have given him an excellent nature, seated him in heavenly places with Christ Jesus and given him the keys to your kingdom (Matthew 18:18). Thank you that you replicate yourself within him and in his circumstances.
AMEN.

151

CONQUEST

1 John 5:4
For everyone who has been born of God overcomes the world.
And this is the victory that has overcome the world - our faith.
(NIV)

MY DECREE

By God's grace, my son is a conqueror and more. Through the gift of faith, my son trusts, hopes, believes, and has full confidence that the Lord is for him and has a perfect plan for his life. The Lord helps my son to be more than a winner in life, regardless of the circumstances he may find himself in. Nothing of this world is controlling my son. Rather, my son is more than a victor through Christ and he prevails over every difficulty. My son is an overcomer.

MY PRAYER

Dear Lord Jesus Christ,
I fear nothing because of you. I thank you for the spiritual gift of faith and ask that you would give me an extra measure of faith at every stage. I ask that in challenging times, the power and might that is in my son will defeat difficult circumstances. I am grateful that my son is mastering and dominating every negative that presents itself before him. Thank you that my son is born of you and because of that he has victory in all walks of life.
AMEN.

152

PREDESTINATION

Jeremiah 1:5
Before I formed you in the womb I knew you, before you were born I set you apart. (NIV)

MY DECREE

The spirit of my son remembers what God has placed within it before he was conceived. Every good thing, talent, skill, gift, blessing, strength, empowerment that God has put my son's name on, is brought to expression every-day and at every opportunity. My son lives out the purpose that the Lord created him for.

MY PRAYER

Gracious and loving Father,
Thank you that my son is predestined in and by you. He finds his being and purpose for life in you. Thank you that you have called him to accomplish extraordinary things in life. Thank you that nothing can erase your blueprint for his life and that success is definitely in his predestination.
Thank you Lord.
AMEN.

153

GIFTEDNESS

James 1:17
Every good and perfect gift is from above from the Father of the heavenly lights, who does not change like shifting shadows.
(NIV)

MY DECREE

My son has been given talent, ability, aptitude, skill and capacity to achieve great things by the Lord. The Lord has perfected all these gifts and opened my sons heart and mind to his capabilities. These blessings from the Lord are constant, firm and steadfast and they are irrevocable.

MY PRAYER

Dear Lord Jesus Christ,
Thank you for being immutable, faithful, reliable, dependable and stable. You forever remain constant and trustworthy. Thank you that your promises over the life of my son are already established in his life. Thank you that by virtue of your loyalty to and love for me, my son is successful academically and in all that he does.
AMEN.

154

HONOUR

Proverbs 21:21
Whoever pursues righteousness and love finds life, prosperity and honour. (NIV)

MY DECREE

My son pursues a godly character and nature, a godly conscience and attitude, godly conduct and action. He acts with patience, kindness, gentleness, and the truth. He does not rejoice in evil or act in a way that brings hurt to those around him. Therefore, through the goodwill of the Lord, he is thriving, flourishing, succeeding and progressing well. My son is self-respecting and this shows in how he respects others in the world around him. My son honours his parents and Gods purposes and plans for his life.

MY PRAYER

Dear Lord Jesus Christ,
By your grace, my son is respectful in all his relationships. He pays reverence where it is due and lives in harmony with others. As a result of this, you reward him with good things. He is treated with fairness and not according to the colour of his skin or the pronunciation of his name. Thank you that he finds favour in all that he does.
AMEN.

155

GOAL GETTING

1 Corinthians 9v24
Do you know that those who run all run, but one receives the prize? Run in such a way that you may obtain it.(NIV)

MY DECREE

My son excavates the greatness within himself for his own sake. He recognises, nurtures and cultivates it to fruition. He focuses on the unique lane that he has been given to run and he runs with focus, strength, momentum and endurance. Through the power of our Lord Jesus Christ, every negative pattern and experience in my son's life, past, present or future is reversed. It all works together for his good.
Every negative categorisation of my son by himself or anyone else is turned into glory and countless testimonies abound.

MY PRAYER

Our faithful Father in heaven,
Thank you that you enable my son to make steady progress and improvement in all that he does. You have given him a keen sense of focus and the strength he needs to endure. Thank you for giving him the stamina needed to keep on advancing in his academics. Thank you that every crooked path in his way is made straight and that all paths grow brighter and brighter for him academically and otherwise.
AMEN.

156

CLOSENESS TO GOD

Zephaniah 3:17
The Lord your God is with you, the Mighty Warrior who saves.
He will take great delight in you; in his love he will no longer
rebuke you, but will rejoice with you in singing. (NIV)

MY DECREE

The Lord Himself sings over my son.
Together with the Lord who surrounds us with songs of victory, I continuously have a new song of praise unto the Lord for the success that is always becoming of my son. The lips of my son have tasted and seen that the Lord is good (Psalm 34:8) and they sing a new song of praise to the Lord. My son uses his voice to express his gifts of supernatural knowledge, understanding, wisdom and they prophesy.

MY PRAYER

Dear Lord Jesus Christ,
Thank you that according to your word, your blood has a voice that speaks better things over us (Hebrews 12:24). Thank you that your mouth sings songs of victory, deliverance, encouragement and love over my son and all areas of his life. In times of discouragement and challenge, I thank you that your voice silences every other negative voice and that he finds peace because of your singing.
AMEN.

157

POSITIVE SPEECH

Job 22:28
Thou shalt also decree a thing, and it shall be established unto thee: and the light shall shine upon thy ways.
(KJV)

MY DECREE

I experience every good thing I say over my son and his academics. I am redeemed and I say so (Psalm 107:2) and I use my lips to say what I would like to see. Therefore I say that he is blessed excellently and that the grace for excellence is in his life. I say that schoolwork, exercises, calculations, examinations, assignments, tests and assessments are all easy for my son and he excels in them. I say that the Lord is with my son and his teachers and they bring out the very best of excellence in him academically and otherwise.

MY PRAYER

Lord Jesus Christ our king,
I thank you that you have made me a royal priesthood and bestowed upon me the honour of being a king. Thank you that through my words I can create life and death and that I can silence and condemn every word spoken against me in judgment. Thank you that I can issue edicts, rules, declarations, injunctions, directives and commands over my son, based on the knowledge of your word. Thank you for authenticating my words when I say that he is blessed, highly favoured, victorious, successful and praiseworthy. His present is bright and his future is brilliant. He is blessed so as to be a blessing at all times.
AMEN.

158

GUIDANCE

Isaiah 58:11
And the Lord will guide you continually and satisfy your desire in scorched places and make your bones strong; and you shall be like a watered garden, like a spring of water, whose waters do not fail. (ESV)

MY DECREE

The Lord places yearnings inside the heart of my son. There is abundant life in his marrow. The Lord grants my sons longings and He exceeds my son's expectations. The Lord provides a light for my son to follow like a compass and it leads to experiences that are brimming with life. This light is in my son's mind, body and in all his activities and circumstances. This is the experience of my son in all seasons.

MY PRAYER

Gracious God,
You have promised that if I focus on you, fast and pray and do good to others around me, you will bless me. I ask that my sacrifices and offerings will come before you and on that basis, that you will bless my son. May you fulfil my desires for him and the generations that are to come from his loins. I pray that you will answer my cries over his life and satisfy me with good news and testimonies. Fill my life with joy because of my son Lord.
AMEN.

159

WELFARE

Isaiah 3:10
Tell the righteous that it shall be well with them, for they shall eat the fruit of their deeds. (NIV)

MY DECREE

My son is part of an ecosystem of good works and admirable conduct. As a result, he matures into a person of good character who lives a morally upright life. Consequentially, good achievements thrive in his life.
My son is willing and doing good to himself in all areas of his life. Those around him respond by doing their best to further his cause.

MY PRAYER

Dear Lord Jesus Christ,
Thank you that you are righteous and just. You are the judge of all things and peoples. I ask that you would grant my son academic success and a godly character and reward me for what I have invested in his growth and development. May this gratuity come in the form of good success for him. I ask that you would be blessed by him and that he will come closer to you because of your love and favour.
AMEN.

160

FAITH

2 Corinthians 5:7
For we live by faith, not by sight. (NIV)

MY DECREE

The Holy Spirit grants the gift of great faith to my son (1 Corinthians 12:9). Christ then gives him an extra measure of faith to live by (Romans 12:3). As a family, we are not moved by what we see with our physical eyes. By faith, I see the goodness of God in every area of my son's life: physically, emotionally, mentally, spiritually and in his soul. I see my son exceling in all that he is doing and this leads to a bright and excellent future. I see him being congratulated and rewarded for brilliance. I see excellent results and our son growing stronger, more confident and better able in all he does.

MY PRAYER

Our faithful father,
I place all of my trust and confidence in you. I am convinced that you continue to keep me in your wonderful will. I have an assurance that you are taking care of my son and that your good plans for him succeed.
I am fully persuaded that your love, kindness, perfection and excellent spirit are reflected in his academics and in every phase of his life. Thank you that the devil is a liar therefore I do not believe any of the lies that I may be told about my son. Neither does he. My faith is in the truth: that your plans are to bless my son academically and otherwise.
AMEN.

GODLY PASSION

Hebrews 11:6
And without faith it is impossible to please Him, for he that cometh to God must believe that he is, and that he is a rewarder of them that diligently seek him. (NKJV)

MY DECREE

I constantly look for and create opportunities to be in the presence of the Lord regarding my son. As I pray for him, I welcome improvement, growth, development and all that is good and perfect, into my sons life. This includes the best achievements, physical and spiritual growth, closeness to God, protection, academic elucidation, rapid physical, mental and spiritual growth.

MY PRAYER

Our heavenly father,
I thank you that I live by faith. I say these prayers and speak out these words in faith as a way of life. I thank you that because you are alive, my son can live in victory. Thank you that you award me with answers to prayer because of my faith. Thank you that by faith, my son achieves academic success and in victory in all areas of his life.
AMEN.

162

SECURITY

Isaiah 54:17
No weapon that is formed against thee shall prosper. (KJV)

MY DECREE

Every mental, physical, psychological, spiritual enemy of my son's progress is defeated. Whatever tries to come against my sons soul, his imagination, heart, spirit and body fails to accomplish its enterprise in his life. The Lord helps my son to renew his mind, to strengthen his emotional core and to be resilient against attack. This results in the transformation of all negativity into good experiences that constantly get better. Every bad word, attitude or idea about my son is exchanged for good and he is thriving at all times.

MY PRAYER

Dear Lord Jesus Christ,
Thank you for dying for me on the cross and declaring that all that was working against me, my seed and fruit is finished. Thank you for disarming my enemy and making a public spectacle of him by your victory on the cross of calvary (Colossians 1:7).
Thank you that by your blood shed on the cross of calvary, I now have reconciliation with the Father and victory in life. You were chastised for my peace and I can confidently declare that my son was included in your victory even then. My victories in Christ are seen in my son's all-round success.
AMEN.

163

ENHANCEMENT

Hebrews 6:9
We are confident that you are meant for better things, things that come with salvation (NLT)

MY DECREE

My son has confessed that Christ is Lord and believed this in his heart. He has therefore accepted the gift of salvation and it is irrevocable. He is due to receive the benefits of this decision. He is also personally working out his own salvation freely. He is sharing his salvation and meets with all that the Lord has appointed for him at any given time. Should he backslide, the seed of his salvation speaks for him and shows him the way back to the Lord. Whenever necessary, he repents and rededicates his life to Christ. So shall it be.

MY PRAYER

Lord Jesus Christ,
By the power of the cross, I and my son have attained deliverance and we are saved. Thank you for the better things that accompany us because we have salvation . I am assured that our lives are filled with blessings and uncommonly positive experiences. The better things that are stated in your word are also reflected in all areas of my son's life. By faith I make this declaration.
AMEN.

164

BLESSED WORKS

Psalm 90:17
May the favour of the Lord our God rest on us; establish the work of our hands - yes confirm the work of our hands. (NIV)

MY DECREE

My son's hands are submitted to the Lord for empowerment and enablement. Whatever they touch and do is blessed and fruitful. They produce good works. He always tries his very best at all times and he does not give up. Every attempt to try to do better is met with reward. The spirit of God empowers my son to keep making a good effort and he reaps good rewards. My son is anointed to work without toiling.

MY PRAYER

Dear Lord Jesus Christ,
Thank you that you have enabled my son to be a smart and diligent worker. I am confident that you will exceed our expectations when you reward his fortitude. Thank you that academically and otherwise, he is always blessed and highly favoured. Thank you for his future that is secure in you.
AMEN.

165

UNIQUENESS

2 Corinthians 4: 7-9
But we have this treasure in jars of clay, to show that the surpassing power belongs to God and not to us. (NIV)

MY DECREE

The Lord placed treasures in my son even before he was born. I believe that they include academic success, excellence, achievements, acclaim, accolades and being discovered and displayed to the world. Moreover, the Lord has given my son hidden treasures that are meant for him. Every teacher and boss is anointed and appointed to help reveal these treasures so that my son and his generation can benefit. My son is a treasure to me and to God and nothing shall be rob him, us or God of this. The wider world recognises and appreciates the treasure he is and the treasure he holds and they respect him while bringing out the best in him.

MY PRAYER

Lord Jesus Christ,
I am grateful for the rich and valuable gifts, callings, talents, abilities and anointings that you have bestowed upon my son. By your spirit, he is fruitful in all areas of his life. I am assured that your power is at work in and through him and that his life is a testimony of your presence and power.
AMEN.

166

EXCELLENCE

Proverbs 22:6
Train up a child in the way he should go, and when he is old he will not depart from it. (ESV)

MY DECREE

I am equipped, through God's grace to train up my son in the way that he should go according to the purposes of the Lord for every stage of his life. I receive from God the training necessary to identify and realise the potential God has placed in my son and entrusted to me.
His teachers and the community around him are doing the same. Where necessary, the Lord provides spiritual parents, brothers and sisters for my son and they lead him aright.

MY PRAYER

Dear Lord Jesus Christ,
Thank you for enabling me to instruct, coach, teach and guide my son in the paths of righteousness. Thank you that his life is evidence of the lessons that you have taught me about him. Thank you that by your grace, my son is rooted and grounded in you, himself and in the Word of God. I am blessed to have him as a son.
AMEN.

167

EXPANSION AND GROWTH

Isaiah 26:15
You have enlarged the nation, LORD; you have enlarged the nation. You have gained glory for yourself; you have extended all the borders of the land. (NIV)

MY DECREE

My son carries the potential to be a nation. Moreover, the Lord has predestined and marked out physical and spiritual territory for him to conquer and possess. In fact, by the favour of God, this province is enlarged, as is the place of my son's influence and success. Every hidden path and doorway to this territory is now illuminated and opened and my son excels in it, beyond measure.

MY PRAYER

Lord, God Almighty,
Thank you that by your grace, you have created a nation out of my son. I thank you for the godly people that will come out of him. They will be people of great purpose and achievement. Thank you that my sons life expands on all sides. I ask you to perpetually increase his territory. May he be a person of influence, academically and otherwise.
AMEN.

168

ABILITY

Philippians 4:13
I can do all things through Christ which strengtheneth me.
(KJV)

MY DECREE

My son passes every evaluative process that he is put through. Failure is not of God or my son and it is not an option in his life. No matter how difficult the test, the Lord will equip my son and he will succeed in it, no matter what, how, who, when or where.
The spirit of wisdom and understanding is at hand to teach him well and my son is enabled to do well.

MY PRAYER

Dear Lord Jesus Christ,
Thank you that you are the strength of my sons life.
There is no limit to what he can do academically and in all areas of life. In you, his abilities are limitless. I decree and declare in your presence that he is a man of valour who continuously accomplishes great things, through your power that is at work in him.
AMEN.

169

RENEWAL

Isaiah 43:19
See, I am doing a new thing! Now it springs up; do you not perceive it? I am making a way in the wilderness and streams in the wasteland.(NIV)

MY DECREE

At every stage and in every day, the Lord is doing something novel in my sons life. The Lords power is always potent and transformative and it works for my son. I am grateful for the new experiences, new gifts, new talents, new networks, new levels of power, strength and wisdom that the Lord is giving him.

MY PRAYER

Dear Lord Jesus,
Your mercies for my son are new every morning. Goodness and mercy follow him all the days of his life. At every turn you are bringing forth fresh blessings and ideas that are appropriate for every situation at hand. I thank you that you constantly open his mind to receive, assimilate and understand the concepts that are introduced to him at every phase. I thank you for the newness of his life every-day and renewed strength.
AMEN.

170

EXCESS

Ephesians 3:20
Now all glory to God, who is able to do immeasurably more than all we ask or imagine, according to his power that is at work within us. (NIV)

MY DECREE

The potential placed by God in my son is unlimited. There is an uncapped grace upon my son for excellence, academically and otherwise. The power of God in my son's life is inexhaustible and it causes him to achieve great things. There is immeasurable power in the name of Jesus Christ to help my son to overcome every enemy to his potential. My son's rise is meteoric.

MY PRAYER

Dear Lord Jesus Christ,
Thank you that you are faithful in all your ways towards my son. Thank you that you are exceeding all of our expectations of and for my son. Thank you that the force and potency of your strength and authority are within him and that they are reflected in his interactions with the world around him at all times.
AMEN.

171

DEVOUTNESS

Genesis 1:27
Put on your new nature, created to be like God – truly righteous and holy. (NIV)

MY DECREE

My son is created in the image and likeness of God, his Father. His spiritual man arises and comes to the fore in all of his experiences and all that he needs to do. He shows forth his true nature as an upright, moral and victorious person in all he does. He does not conform to the nature and standards of this world. Rather, he reflects a Christ-like mind and he is set apart in a class that God has put him in. He is ever victorious, ever buoyant, ever fruitful, ever resourceful and ever potent. There is no challenge too big for him.

MY PRAYER

Dear Lord Jesus Christ,
Thank you that, according to your word, my son is a copy and replica of you. Thank you that your characteristics, traits, wisdom, holiness and power are reflected through him. Thank you that he knows you intimately and is manifesting the divine nature that you made him in to himself and the world around him.
AMEN.

172

UNDERSTANDING

Proverbs 2:6
For the Lord gives wisdom, from his mouth cometh knowledge and understanding. (KJV)

MY DECREE

By the spirit of the Lord, my son understands all that is required of him at every stage. He is aware of his responsibilities and he knows how to carry them out. He easily acquires and retains knowledge. By his God-given intelligence, judgment and discernment, he makes the right choices. My son lives, moves and has his being in the Lord (Acts 17:28).

MY PRAYER

Dear Lord Jesus Christ,
Thank you that you have bestowed an uncommon grace for insight, sound judgment and intellect in my son. Thank you that he is well informed and is applying reason in all of his affairs. Thank you that he confidently grasps the lessons of life and academia with ease and applies them in his life and interactions with those around him.
AMEN.

173

CONQUEST

1 John 5:4
For every child of God defeats this evil world, and we achieve this victory through our faith. (NLT)

MY DECREE

The Lord guarantees my son victory over sin, failure and every negative experience. My son overcomes all challenges to his progress. Victory is his in Christ Jesus and the Lord himself surrounds him with songs of victory, now and in the future (Zephaniah 3:17).

MY PRAYER

Dear Lord Jesus Christ,
Thank you that you have already overcome the world so that I can fear not. Thank you that regardless of the afflictions that my son may go through, he is delivered from every one of them. Thank you that the spirit that makes people achieve great things with ease is also in him. Thank you for giving my son the ability to master every challenge so that he is achieving success in every test and trial. In your name I pray,
AMEN.

174

ORDINATION

Psalm 139:13-14
For you created my inmost being; you knit me together in my mother's womb. I praise you because I am fearfully and wonderfully made; your works are wonderful, I know that full well. (NIV)

MY DECREE

The Lord has been intimate with my son since his conception and knows him intricately. All of Gods creations are good and perfect and so is my son, including in his mind, body, heart, soul and spirit. My son is therefore holy and set apart for the Lord who created him. There is an unquantifiable and immeasurable valuation of my son's life and his future. He is celebrated in heaven and the earth blesses him. My son is an esteemed member of every sector of society. He is valued in our family and wherever he goes he is embraced, welcomed and accepted.

MY PRAYER

Dear Lord Jesus Christ,
Thank you that the greatness with which you created my son is shining through him. Thank you that every gift, calling and blessing that you have woven in him is holding his life together. Thank you that you have prepared magnificent things for him and that he shows forth an excellent spirit.
Thank you for showing forth your magnificence through him.
AMEN.

175

PRAYER

Jeremiah 33:3
Call to me and I will answer you, and will tell you great and hidden things that you have not known. (ESV)

MY DECREE

My son is hearing and heeding the voice of God in his life. This voice is unmistakable, clear and audible. My son articulates and declares the word of God while also raising his voice in prayer and praise to God and against evil. Every expression that is not of the Lord is silenced and my son does not hear or listen to it.

MY PRAYER

Dear Lord Jesus Christ,
Thank you that your voice is amplified in my sons life and that it silences every other negative voice speaking to and about him, whether inside himself or in the world around him. Thank you for unlocking and illuminating the mysteries of life to him and showing him the paths of righteousness and excellence. Thank you for the voice of your word and the words of your voice to him. Thank you for leading and guiding him every step of the way in his life.
AMEN.

176

TESTIMONIALS

Psalm 40:5
O LORD my God, you have performed many wonders for us. Your plans for us are too numerous to list. You have no equal. If I tried to recite all your wonderful deeds, I would never come to the end of them. (NLT)

MY DECREE

I am grateful that the Lord has done great miracles on my son's behalf and they have brought astounding success. The Lord has programs, arrangements, schemes and schedules that benefit my son at all stages of his life. He has anointed and appointed people to be a blessing to my son. The Lord has predestined and equipped my son to achieve good purposes. Nothing stifles the intentions of the Lord for my son.

MY PRAYER

Dear Lord Jesus Christ,
Thank you that everything you allow in my sons life is intentional and purposeful. Thank you that your deeds in his life bring amazement and wonderment to me and the world around him. Thank you for all your aspirations for him. By faith, I thank you that they are unfolding daily. Thank you that blessings and miracles follow each other in his life and that he is a wonder because of you.
AMEN.

DIVINE SUCCESS

Ecclesiastes 5:19
Moreover, when God gives someone wealth and possessions, and the ability to enjoy them, to accept their lot and be happy in their toil-this is a gift of God. (NIV)

MY DECREE

My son constantly receives wisdom from the Lord and it brings wealth and riches to him. My son lacks nothing and lives in a realm of excess and he is a blessing to others. Moreover, he is enabled to rest and delight in the work of his hands. He is willing to keep on exceling and to take pleasure in the fruits of his hands. He develops the right character. He identifies and exploits opportunities. Because of his character he continues to rise and enjoy promotion. He does not borrow and he does not go into debt.

MY PRAYER

Dear Lord Jesus Christ,
Thank you for the good fortune that you have bestowed upon my son. Thank you that the intellect and acumen of his mind, spirit and soul cause him to live out the abundant life that you came to give him. Thank you for the abundance of human and other resources that are available to him at every stage. Thank you for the rest that you give him and the recreation that he is enjoying while being rejuvenated and restored by your spirit. Thank you that he is showing forth wonderful fruits from his labour and enjoying them with his loved ones.
AMEN.

178

INSIGHT

Proverbs 4:6-7
Do not forsake wisdom, and she will protect you, love her, and she will watch over you. The beginning of wisdom is that: Get wisdom. Though it cost all you have, get understanding. (NIV)

MY DECREE

My son is blessed with an innate spirit of wisdom that is imbibed in him by God, from conception. It is also granted to him as an additional spiritual gift and it works with prudence, knowledge and understanding of physical and spiritual matters. My son therefore lives a long and good life filled with riches and honour, power and peace.

MY PRAYER

Our Father in Heaven, I am grateful that my son walks in uncommon measures of understanding, knowledge, prudence, intelligence and wise judgment. Thank you that he is excelling in mind, body and soul at all times in his life. Thank you for the spirit of discernment and reason that you have given him. In the name of Jesus Christ I pray,
AMEN.

179

SUPPORT

3 John 1:2
Beloved, I wish above all things that thou mayest prosper and be in good health, even as your soul prospereth. (KJV)

MY DECREE

There is uncommon wealth and vitality in my sons soul, mind and spirit. This results in progress, success, advancement, increase and abundance in his affairs. He lives in a realm of mental, spiritual and physical wealth. His mind, will and emotions are well-regulated, strong, fertile, fruitful and full of vigour.

MY PRAYER

Dear Lord Jesus Christ,
Thank you for the treasures in the soul of my son and that it is thriving. Thank you that he is making good progress and he advances on all sides. Thank you that he is growing, developing and blossoming in all areas of his life, mind, could, spirit and heart. Thank you for the physical manifestation of this in all of his surroundings and circumstances.
AMEN.

180

ILLUMINATION

Isaiah 54:12
And I will make your towers of sparkling rubies, your gates of shining gems, and your walls of precious stones. (ESV)

MY DECREE

The Lord gives my son the physical and spiritual treasures of the earth. Portals of revelation, light, knowledge, wisdom, learning and elucidation are open to my son. They bring him great success. His steps give him to access into uncommon possibilities and riches and these blessings set him apart.

MY PRAYER

Dear Lord Jesus,
Thank you for being the foundation, cornerstone, capstone and pillar that holds my son's life together and keeps it standing. Thank you for the lessons that you are teaching my son. May they enable him to access the riches of the earth and your kingdom. Thank you that you are constantly promoting him to greater realms of revelation and wisdom and that they are permitting him to enjoy the best that life has to offer.
AMEN.

181

PROVISION

Psalm 23:1
The Lord is my shepherd, I lack nothing. (NIV)

MY DECREE

The Lord leads, guides, steers, shadows, accompanies and pastors my son at all times. My son is helped and aided, attended to an chaperoned by the Lord. He enjoys the resources, provision, endowments, supplies and facilities of the kingdom of God. These are spiritually, emotionally, mentally, psychologically and physically available to my son at all times. He is kept from harm, scarcity, need and deficiency. Instead, he receives opportunities, success, glory, help, assistance, protection and provision. Understanding, godly friendships, respect, good health, longevity, rest, relaxation and recreation are an integral part of his life. My son lives a life of empowerment, enablement, accomplishment and victory. Every good thing that pertains to life, academics and godliness is freely exploited and enjoyed by my son.

MY PRAYER

Dear Lord God,
Thank you for being the Good Shepherd in my sons life. Thank you that you feed him, you show him the way to go, protect him and guard over all aspects of his life. Thank you for your watchful eye over him and that you neither slumber nor sleep. Thank you for constantly watching him and tending to his affairs. Thank you that you identify his needs and open up your hand to feed him and that you gently lead him in the way that he should go. Thank you also for correcting him and bringing him back into the fold whenever he goes astray.
AMEN.

182

BIBLICAL KNOWLEDGE

Hebrews 4:12
For the word of God is alive and active. Sharper than any double-edged sword, it penetrates even to dividing soul and spirit, joints and marrow; it judges the thoughts and attitudes of the heart. (NIV)

MY DECREE

The word of God dwells in my son and in his heart and brings him life. It is awake, quick, energetic, swift and effective in my son's life. My words over him are influencing and transforming all the circumstances that he is surrounded by at any given time, including right now. Every negative word spoken over, about and to my son is of no effect. Every word of failure from my son or anyone else isnot of God. It is a lie and it has no life.

MY PRAYER

Dear Lord Jesus Christ, I thank you for the potency of your word spoken about my son. Thank you that your word is cutting through and cutting out every negative experience from his mind, body, soul and spirit. Thank you that your word is the sword of the spirit (Ephesians 6:17) and that it produces compelling victories in my sons life.
AMEN.

183

LIBERATION

2 Corinthians 3:17
Now the Lord is the spirit, and where the Spirit of the Lord is, there is freedom. (ESV)

MY DECREE

My son is liberated from any realm of evil. He is emancipated from anything ungodly that seeks his life and his mind. He is delivered, loosed, unchained and disentangled from anything that does not bring glory to the name of Jesus Christ. My son is released, liberated and discharged from the influences, control and works of Satan and anyone or anything he uses. My son identifies all workers of iniquity from afar and his path does not cross with theirs.

MY PRAYER

Dear Lord Jesus Christ, I worship you because your spirit brings liberation, independence, autonomy and self-determination to my son. Thank you that your spirit is ever present and with him at all times and in all places. Because of your nearness, he will always have freedom permanently.
AMEN.

184

ENDEAVOUR

. Romans 12:11
Never be lazy, but work hard and serve the Lord enthusiastically. (NLT)

MY DECREE

My son is diligent, enterprising, energetic, enthusiastic and industrious in all things. He is a smart worker who is productive. He is spirited and spurred on by the effervescence of the Spirit of the Lord. He achieves much spiritually and physically using his mind, heart and soul. The Lord uses him to accomplish much for his kingdom and in his community.

MY PRAYER

Dear Lord Jesus Christ,
I praise you because my son is steadfast and ever potent in all he does. Thank you that encouragement, motivation and empowerment rise up in him at all times. Thank you that he is always working for, through and with you in all the areas of his life.
AMEN.

185

CAREFULNESS

Psalm 118:23
This is the Lords doing and it is wonderful to see. (NLT)

MY DECREE

My son is always focused on his academic work, on Christ and on his calling and purpose for life. He attains and achieves all God's desires for him. Greatness manifests in him early and I rejoice over him at every step on his way to maturity. I am well pleased with his progress. The Lord continues to achieve wonders through him.

MY PRAYER

Dear Lord,
Thank you that you have done marvellous things in, through and for my son. Thank you that your presence and acts in his life bring me pride and joy. I am encouraged and motivated to love you more because of how you have blessed me through my son.
AMEN.

186

PERSONAL GODLINESS

Psalm 116:16
Truly I am your servant, Lord: I serve you just as my mother did; you have freed me from my chains (NIV).

MY DECREE

Through my prayers and the grace of the Lord Jesus Christ, my son emulates me in my love for the Lord and prayer. The same Father that has called me to pray and seek His face also imparts the same anointing on my son as a generational blessing. By Gods favour, my son is closer to the Lord Jesus Christ than his mother is or ever was. Every fetter, restraint, bond and lock on his life is broken along with anything that is not of the glory of God in him.

MY PRAYER

Dear Lord Jesus, I thank you that through your infinite love for my son and I, you have a close and personal relationship with him. Thank you that his relationship with you is based on his personal experiences with you and from there, it passes on to future generations.
AMEN.

187

CONSCIENCE

1 Timothy 1:5
The purpose of this (the Lord's) order is to arouse the love that comes from a pure heart, a clear conscience and a genuine faith.

MY DECREE

My son is at peace with man and God at all times. He is patient, kind and loving to all and the Lord cleanses his heart from all that is ungodly. He exhibits a reverent nature and character in all that he does. He lives in peace with all creation and the Lord gives him extra measures of faith. The Lord Jesus Christ is the inner voice that guides my son and blesses him with good principles, standards and ethics.

MY PRAYER

Lord Jesus Christ, I am grateful for your grace and mercy in the life of my son. I thank you that since God is love, that love is exhibited inside of my son. The love of God helps my son to love himself in a godly way and to love life and those around him. I thank you that his heart is clean and it meditates only on that which is good and positive. Thank you that his soul is healed and brimming with health and that his spirit is always clean.
AMEN.

WILL

Philippians 2:13
For God is working in you, giving you the desire and the power to do what pleases him. (NLT)

MY DECREE

My son's attitude, behaviour and character are submitted to the Lord. Due to the fact that the Holy Spirit dwells in him, he acts in a way that blesses the Lord and the world around him. My son is yielding to the Lord and has committed his thoughts and actions to the Lord. By the power that is at work in my son's spirit, he carries out the pleasurable and good purposes of the Lord in his generation and beyond.

MY PRAYER

Dear Lord Jesus Christ, I thank you that the holy spirit is resident inside of my son's life. I thank you that through the leading of the holy spirit and His guidance at all times, my son develops a godly attitude, behaviour and character that is pleasing to you, to us, his generation and all those who come into contact with him. I pray that you would be gratified and satisfied with him.
AMEN.

PURPOSE

Psalm 33:11
But the plans of the Lord stand firm forever, the purposes of his heart through all generations (NIV).

MY DECREE

My son and I receive generational blessings from the Lord and we pass these on to generations that are to come. Through us, the Lord ministers to current and future generations. We find our place in the five-fold ministry of the Lord and function to the maximum of our abilities in our chosen role in the kingdom of our God. We are forever blessed because the Lord is mindful of us.

MY PRAYER

Dear Lord Jesus Christ,
I thank you that you have good plans for my son: to prosper him in all of his ways, in accordance with your word, will and power. I thank you that there may be many plans that I and others make for my son, but it is only your purposes that stand forever (Proverbs 19:21). Thank you that this is true for my son and I and for generations to come.
AMEN.

190

MENTAL HEALTH

2 Timothy 1:7
For God has not given us a spirit of fear, but of power and of love and a sound mind. (NKJV)

1 Peter 5:7
Cast all your anxiety on Him because he cares for you. (NIV)

MY DECREE

My son has the mind of Christ (1 Corinthians 2:16). No weapon formed over his mind will prosper because my son has a positive mindset, self-concept and self-esteem. Every negative stronghold in the form of a memory, mentality, psychology, frame and state of mind and psych. He is not anxious or fearful. He was prayed for before conception and within the womb and he came from God, therefore his mind is incorruptible. The fire of the Lord consumes all anger, agitation and all forms of emotional or mental disorders. Everything in his mind is ordered and aligned to the peace of the Lord and it guards his heart and mind in Christ Jesus. The hand of the Lord Jesus Christ uproots all forms of stress and trauma from my sons psychological make-up and the blood of Jesus Christ washes his mind clean.

MY PRAYER

Dear Lord, like Hannah did with Samuel, I place my son back into your hands. I thank you that the power of your and my love and light is able to save and rescue my son from all mental anguish. Thank you that the brilliance of his mind is manifesting in the name of the Lord Jesus Christ. He will accomplish everything that you predestined him to do. I am grateful that my son achieves and attains everything that you have set out for him in a timeous way that is not delayed. Thank you for preparing him to function in your purpose and calling over his life.
AMEN.

191

GOD'S COUNSEL

Jeremiah 23:18
For who among them has stood in the council of the Lord to see and to hear his word, or who had paid attention to his word and listened? (NIV)

MY DECREE

By the blessing of the Lord, my son is keen to stand before the Lord so as to see and hear what the Lord is speaking at any given time. He has the peace of mind and heart to sustain a conversation with the Lord and to receive guidance on how to proceed at every juncture of his life. The Lord who made the eye and the ear is communicating with my son in audible visions, dreams and other means that serve to provide guidance to him.

MY PRAYER

Dear Lord,
I thank you that my son is made in your image and likeness. This means that he is hearing and understanding you when you communicate with him. I am thankful that you who created the ear is speaking your counsel into his ear for him to hear you. Thank you that he is coming to a place and time where your word is imbibed inside his heart and that it brings light into his soul.
AMEN.

192

SPIRITUAL SONSHIP

Romans 8:15
For you did not receive the spirit of slavery to fall back into fear, but you have received the Spirit of adoption as sons, by who we cry, "Abba! Father!" (NIV)

MY DECREE

By the grace of our Lord Jesus Christ, my son is a child of God. As such, he enjoys the inheritance that has been set aside for him by the Lord. By God's grace, the Holy Spirit who bestows gifts on men gives my son the spirit of grace and supplication as well as all the spiritual gifts recorded in the Bible. I am grateful that the Lord inclines his ears to my son.

MY PRAYER

Dear Lord, I am grateful that you are always with my son at all times so he has no cause to be afraid. I pray that he will know and sense your presence at all times and without the shadow of a doubt. I ask that as an expression of your grace and favour, you will give him an extra measure of the kind of faith that subdues fear. I thank you that his faith, even if it is as small as a mustard seed, continues to grow.
AMEN.

193

SPIRTUAL FRUITFULNESS

Galatians 5:22
But the fruit of the Spirit is love, joy, peace, patience, kindness, goodness, faithfulness (NIV).

MY DECREE

I praise the Lord that the holy spirit lives and abides inside of my son. I thank the Lord that the spirit of the Lord is not barren, but bears multiple fruits. By faith, through every situation and circumstance, the Lord is planting and cultivating the right seeds inside of my son and these yield good results in my son's attitude, behaviour and character as well in every area of his life, work and existence.

MY PRAYER

Dear Lord,
I thank you that God is love and that, no matter what, my son is an embodiment of love. This love is for himself, for his family and the wider world. I thank you that by your help, my son is patient and kind to himself and others. Thank you that he is loved in return and that through that love, he deepens his consciousness of and relationship with you.
AMEN.

194

PEACE

John 14:27
Peace I leave with you; my peace I give to you. Not as the world gives do I give to you. Let not your hearts be troubled, neither let them be afraid (NIV).

MY DECREE

An incomprehensible peace resides in my son. It is cultivated by the Holy Spirit who always comforts and calms him. This peace reassures him in times of difficulty, discomfort, growth, development and stress. It lifts him up to a realm where he functions well and accomplishes all that is required of him, in-spite of the circumstances.

MY PRAYER

Dear Lord,
I thank you that you are an embodiment of peace and that you dwell inside of my son. May your peace within him radiate into his daily affairs and interactions. By that peace, may he excel. I thank you that it is your peace that strengthens him and helps him to identify and pursue his life's purpose and to achieve much.
AMEN.

195

SOUL

Psalm 23:3
He restores my soul, He leads me in the paths of righteousness for his names sake (NIV).

MY DECREE

The spirit of my son is prospering at all times.
His mind, will and emotions are always in alignment with Gods purpose for him. Because his soul is thriving he is enjoying peace and power.
He makes the best decisions and arises to every occasion, meeting every demand and overcoming every challenge. When things get difficult, his soul is restored and renewed with more life and strength and this enables him to accomplish much.

MY PRAYER

Dear Lord,
I thank you that my son is your son.
Thank you that because you are righteous and powerful, so is my son.
I thank you that his feet are anointed and appointed to walk in paths of goodness and uncommon realms of glory.
I pray that by your grace, you direct him to your house and altar and that his feet carry him into your presence.
AMEN.

196

SPIRIT

Psalm 51:10
Create in me a clean heart, O God, and renew a right spirit within me (NIV).

MY DECREE

The Lord forms a pure and unpolluted heart inside my son. He fills it with strength, purity, positivity and good thoughts. My sons heart is incorruptible. By God's grace, all thoughts of darkness are cleaned out of my sons consciousness and his psyche by the blood of Jesus Christ. My sons spirit is strong, buoyant, renewed, vibrant, enthusiastic and powerful. It constantly springs forth, brimming with life and a zest for living.

MY PRAYER

Dear Lord Jesus Christ,
I am grateful that you are speaking to my son in his heart at any given time. I thank you that the Holy Spirit within my son is renewing and replenishing his spirit. Thank you that my son is walking in the right paths that you have predestined for him. I bless you for helping the spirit of my son to produce good in his and our lives. May his heart always be full of vitality and powerful energy that he uses it for good. I pray that even in times of weariness and discouragement, he will still hear the spirit of the Lord within him.
AMEN.

197

PATH

Psalm 143:10
You are my God; teach me to do your will. Be good to me, and guide me on a safe path (NIV)

MY DECREE

I am grateful that the Lord is the father of my son.
I thank the Lord that Jesus Christ is a teacher and I hold on to the promise that my son is taught of the Lord and his peace is great.
I praise the Lord that He serves as the compass that leads my son along the paths that he should follow, according to the plan of God for his life.
The spirit of the Lord orbits around my son and protects him and his mind from attack.

MY PRAYER

Dear Lord Jesus Christ,
I thank you that you have chosen to love and father my son.
Thank you that through your holy spirit, my son is discerning your ultimate will at any and all times.
Thank you for your goodness and mercy that follow my son wherever he goes. Thank you also that the Holy Spirit is leading my son on the paths of life and righteousness and that these paths grow brighter and brighter on a daily basis.
AMEN.

LIFE

Psalm 16:11
You make known to me the path of life; you will fill me with joy in your presence, with eternal pleasures at your right hand (NIV).

MY DECREE

Holy Spirit leads my son along the path of life. My son walks on it daily with eagerness and joy. Jesus Christ is in front, at the back, to left and to the right of my son. Moreover, my son receives power as he walks with the Lord on this path. He is purposed by the Lord Jesus Christ to see and hear the supernatural for the kingdom of God. He is equipped and refreshed by the Lord along this path. This is reflected in my sons behaviour and comportment as well as his plans and decisions. Evidence of this walk with God is clear in every area of my son's life.

MY PRAYER

Dear Lord Jesus Christ,
I am grateful that you are giving my son an unmistakable encounter with the Holy Spirit. I thank you that as he walks along, the Lord is leading him in the paths of life and the paths of righteousness. I thank the Lord that the joy of the Lord is upon my son like a mantle and that joy is full and complete. I thank you that the pleasures, treasures and benefits that are due to my son from the throne of God are released to him as he walks these paths with the Holy Spirit.
AMEN.

199

COMFORT

2 Corinthians 1:3-4
Praise be to the God and Father of our Lord Jesus Christ, the Father of compassion and the God of all comfort, who comforts us in all our troubles so that we can comfort those in any trouble with the comfort we ourselves received from God
(NIV)

MY DECREE

I praise the Lord that he is compassionate and he shows comfort, grace and favour to my son at all times. I am grateful that at every point of any hurt, sadness and sorrow, my son receives the comfort of the Holy Spirit. In return, my son ministers hope and comfort to the people that he meets so that they also benefit from it. My son will never commit suicide. He defeats depression, anxiety and all other attacks over his mind and destiny.

MY PRAYER

Dear Lord Jesus Christ,
I am grateful for every situation that my son has been through and everything he is going through. Thank you for the capacity that you are building within him to become a minister of hope, comfort and healing to those that need it. Thank you that he effectively and meaningfully touches the lives of other people in a positively life-changing way and he is impacting them the way that you have impacted him.
AMEN

MERCY

Psalm 23:6
Surely your goodness and mercy will follow me all the days of my life, and I will dwell in the house of the Lord forever (NIV).

MY DECREE

The mercies of the Lord over my son are new every morning. They are replenished and multiplied daily. The goodness of God over my sons life is inexhaustible and the grace of God over him is boundless. This reality leads my son to the house of God where he finds and cultivates his own faith.

MY PRAYER

Dear Lord Jesus Christ,
I am grateful for the love that you have for my son.
I am confident that, by faith, your love works with grace, mercy, goodness, kindness, patience, endurance and your providence and together, they work for the good of my son.
AMEN

Made in the USA
Columbia, SC
19 August 2023